Brenda M Wright

THE USE OF PRAYING

The Use of Praying

J. Neville Ward

EPWORTH PRESS

FIRST PUBLISHED 1967
BY
THE EPWORTH PRESS

Book Steward: Frank H. Cumbers

Fernley Hartley Lecture 1967

Printed in Great Britain by
Latimer, Trend & Co. Ltd, Plymouth

IN MEMORY OF MY FATHER

AND FOR

JOY, CHRISTOPHER AND MARK

Pour comprendre le monde, il faut parfois se détourner; pour mieux servir les hommes, les tenir un moment à distance. Mais où trouver la solitude nécessaire à la force, la longue respiration où l'esprit se rassemble et la courage se mesure?

ALBERT CAMUS, L'Été, p. 13

Contents

Preface

I would not have accepted the kind but unwise invitation of the Fernley Hartley Trust to give the 1967 Lecture had I not discovered that the Lecture was originally instituted with benevolent rather than academic intent, to give Methodist ministers unknown in the world of theological or pastoral literature the opportunity of publication.

Accordingly this book does not claim a place within the profound and extensive literature of the spiritual life as the Church catholic so deeply and interestingly understands it. It constitutes principally what I have been trying to teach and preach during thirty years in the circuit ministry, helped of course by such reading and thinking as I have managed to find time to do in the ministerial life.

I owe most to my father, the Rev. John Ward, who was a quiet, persistent presence of prayer and godly peace in the family into which God mercifully called me into being. I remember him as a man who walked with God, who greatly enjoyed life and this, I think, because his existence was ordered from within. As I grew up in his company I became aware of some of the price that has to be paid for such order and joy, and that this is not to be questioned.

My debt to many writers is huge, and some acknowledgement of this is made in the footnotes. I have found D. Z. Phillips's *The Concept of Prayer* a particularly helpful and congenial book, both for his comments on some of the perennial problems of Christian prayer and because I have myself been much helped by two writers whom he apparently finds extremely sympathetic, Dostoevsky and Simone Weil. I must admit that I think Dostoevsky makes too much protest about the tears of a little child and that I find Simone Weil's understanding of humility to be just slightly tainted with what looks to me like masochism, but I share Mr. Phillips's estimate of the importance of the contribution

9

Preface

these writers have made to Christianity's self-understanding.

And there is a debt that I can never repay to the Society of St. John the Evangelist at Oxford who for many years have most kindly welcomed me for my annual Retreat and given me continuing spiritual counsel. Their community house in Marston Street is one of the places where it has seemed to me to be easy to pray.

In this book I have incorporated some material previously used in articles published in *The Preacher's Quarterly*, and I am grateful to the Editor, the Rev. Gordon S. Wakefield, for permission to do this.

J. NEVILLE WARD

16 Hinde Street,
London, W.1.
June 1967

1

Praying and the Community of Faith

No one knows how frequently Jesus prayed. Christian spirituality has built up a tradition of the rightness of regular daily private prayer and has used scripture references to the prayer life of Jesus and other biblical figures to support this tradition, but how much of it had a place in the religious life of Jesus we shall never know. It is argued from probability that 'no day in the life of Jesus passed without the three times of prayer' (morning, afternoon and night).[1] But the gospel records are so scanty that we are in no position to say what Jesus did or did not do regularly. We are accustomed to thinking of him as a man of prayer but this is not a fact that strikes us immediately when we read his life as it does when we read the lives of many Christian saints and holy men of other religions.

There is clear evidence that he taught his disciples one prayer —a characteristically brief and simple prayer yet so full of meaning that a whole life of prayer could be built on it, but there is no evidence that he gave them any extended instruction on the life of prayer as is found in the huge Christian literature of the subject. He certainly was once reproached that he did *not* pray and fast like John the Baptist's followers but enjoyed good company. His disciples may have been concerned about this. We find that once after they had had clear proof that he did in fact pray they asked him to teach them to pray as John taught his disciples. It is not clear whether this means 'Teach us to pray because it obviously means so much to you' or 'Teach us a prayer of our own because this is what the other recognized holy man in the locality is doing, this is what men of God are supposed to do'.

Many Christian people think of prayer as something that religious people are supposed to do. It would be difficult to find a more unfortunate approach. It is impossible to explore the world of prayer with interest and hope of discovery if you feel guilty

[1] J. Jeremias, *The Prayers of Jesus* (London 1967) p. 75.

because you do not pray or when you do not pray. The subject never comes alive to guilt but it does to curiosity and interest. It is worth while admitting that it is quite possible to get along without prayer if 'getting along' means living life with a reasonable amount of happiness and without excessive regret. Many people must do just this, and many Christians among them. But as soon as people experience, with some intensity of inwardness, the wish to live life in the Christian way and at the depth the New Testament recommends, that is to say, to live with a certain attitude to life and certain wishes for it and oneself, to develop a certain way of 'taking it' and reflecting on it, and, particularly, to acquire openness to experience and readiness for it so that life can be loved, prayer then becomes a possibility and has a real chance of becoming a desire. Until people want to pray and are interested in finding out how Christians have most deeply thought about it, it never emerges from the dreary company of 'things I suppose I ought to do'.

Of course, every believer's religious life is partly formed by temperamental characteristics. It may be that certain temperaments will never be interested in private prayer. Some of the recent radical criticism of traditional teaching and practice may come from people who are in fact temperamentally disinclined. This does not mean that their work should be disregarded. Their pleading for new forms and words for expressing the prayer of twentieth-century believers is opportune and one hopes it will stimulate experiment. But it seems that certain personalities will never find private prayer congenial and it is hard to justify the view that they must go on trying. Much of God's will has been done by people who have never found themselves able to pray in the traditional forms. However, some of the radical criticism of traditional Christian prayer overlooks the fact that there is an extensive literature written by people who have liked prayer, believed in it and studied it deeply. Everyone should look at some of this and see if he does not feel the stirring of some desire for that unvisited, or lost, domain of religious life in which so many admirable and interesting people have lived so importantly.

Even believers who have no preliminary problems of this kind but very keenly want their lives refreshed and stimulated and kept authentically Christian by prayer at times begin to wonder whether they have misjudged themselves, because again and again this interest dies. It may survive at some inaccessible depth of the self but all they can observe is that the life has gone out of their prayers. To hear the words of the Collect 'we to whom Thou hast given a hearty desire to pray' is disturbing and mystifying. That is exactly, as far as they can see, what God has not given them.

But the words of the Collect provoke different thoughts if we ask who is the 'we' to whom God is supposed to have given a hearty desire to pray. As Christians understand prayer it is the Church that has been given this desire, rather than ourselves as individual believers.

If we pray at all it is because we have been brought into a praying community. And if we do not pray at all we are, if we are members of the Church, still part of a community that prays. This idea of a community of faith is fundamental in the Christian religion, and it is a characteristic in which Christianity importantly differs from much of the religion that exists alongside it in this world of many religions. Christian prayer is not constituted by the totality of adoration and gratitude and request offered by all Christians in their individuality but by that which they do together as this or that part of the catholic Church. And the principal thing they do together as a community is the liturgy— the official worship of the whole local community of believers. The central and representative part of the liturgy (so central that in much of Christendom this is now what the word 'liturgy' means) is the Eucharist. The Church was in the first instance *asked* to do this, but from very shortly after the first Easter it found itself *wanting* to do this, as though Jesus mysteriously passed to it the desire with which he so strongly desired to eat that Passover with his friends as his final day gathered itself in and darkness came. The hearty desire to pray in this particular way has remained with the Church ever since, sometimes weakening of course, but never completely lost, again and again burning up, like a fire whose withered ashes deceive you into thinking it is out, and in our time a flame of increasing power.

It is in the Eucharist that Christians know that the Church has in fact been given a hearty desire to pray. And our membership in the Church gives us participation in that desire whatever the condition of our faith at any particular time.

And it is in the Eucharist that one sees most clearly what

13

prayer really is in the Christian tradition. It begins and ends in thanking and offering.

Private prayer is a secondary thing. That is not to say that it is not important but simply that it is derivative. It is a continuation of the common prayer of the believing community into the particular life of the individuals who compose it. It is the Church's thanking and offering translated into terms of the individual life each one of us is living.[1] We are never allowed to forget that the body comes first and the member second. The pattern Christian prayer, the Lord's Prayer, is always said in the first person plural even when we are alone,[2] so that it is *we* who pray, the Church of Christ, not the isolated ego in its lonely desire and fear. We ask for the daily bread and deliverance and forgiveness as from within the family of God; so that part of the very act of praying is to put one's needs and desires in a larger setting, alongside the needs of the whole believing community and ultimately of the whole family of man, alongside God's purpose in the Church and the world. This inevitably affects the matter of the prayer. Prayer is a purification and ordering of desire. As the Eucharist is a *sacrifice* of prayer and thanksgiving, so our own private praying is a sacrifice, an offering of our desires to God with the readiness to have God's purpose in the Church and the world modify them, sometimes destroy them, if our getting what we want would not serve the purpose of God.

In this last sense, to pray may well be literally to sacrifice—to give up that part of one's desiring ego for which there cannot be found room in the kingdom of God.

Private prayer is a secondary affair, but it is not expendable. It is possible to emphasize the priority of the liturgy so much that it becomes difficult to find a reason for private prayer.[3] But the liturgy is by nature impersonal, not in the sense that it has no personal reality but because it is communal. There is little place for the individual's private wishes and particular concerns. The form of worship there is decided by the tradition of the Church. The worshipper enters into it most fully and gives most to it and receives most from it when he detaches himself from his personal

---

[1] J. Burnaby, *Soundings* (Ed. Vidler) (Cambridge, 1962), p. 235.

[2] Raissa Maritain, *Notes sur le Pater*, p. 28.

[3] This seems to me the weakness of the otherwise useful introduction to prayer, *This World and Prayer* by Sister Edna Mary (S.P.C.K.).

desires and anxieties and allows his heart to beat with the rhythm of the heart of the Church. This is in part how public worship does what it is meant to do—deliver us from ourselves and turn our minds to God as the great Christian tradition has struggled and suffered to work out what God is and what he is not.[1]

But the individual has the right to be, and needs the means of being, himself before God. He has to live with himself anyway, and he wants to do this with God if possible. Private prayer is the means of completely personal life in God's presence. Most Christians cannot make progress without it. And the more use they make of it, the fuller their participation in public worship. But, once again, they need the liturgy to reintroduce them to what the Church considers prayer rightly to be, and to save their private prayers from sentimentality, self-centredness and superstition.[2]

It is true that some people, for temperamental reasons, will always find private prayer infinitely less worth while than public prayer, but there are others, many others, who need encouragement to attempt their own adventure in prayer, because this is going to be their principal means of grace without which they will spiritually die. Among Methodists this is particularly true in the contemporary decline of preaching, a decline so devastating that most Methodists now are reaching the exasperation long since reached by Anglicans and Roman Catholics in which one expects little from the sermon and too often finds this expectation justified.

Another familiar criticism of prayer comes from those who argue the redundancy of prescribed forms of prayer and places of prayer because they can pray just as well walking in the country, or on a deserted beach by some quiet sea evocative of the infinite, or at a rugger match, or at one's work.

But prayer is always to be understood in terms of the religious tradition in which it is offered.[3] A Buddhist monk at prayer is doing what is understood by prayer in the Buddhist tradition. A Christian at prayer is doing what is regarded as prayer in the Christian religion, if it is the instructed and adult Christian in him who is praying and not some lazy or neurotic self; that is to say, he is affirming, expressing, deepening his dependence on

[1] Romano Guardini, *L'Initiation à la Prière* (Editions Alsatia), pp. 234–5.
[2] Op. cit., p. 242.
   Cf. D. Z. Phillips, *The Concept of Prayer*, pp. 36–7.

God and his desire for God's kingdom. Christian prayer arises from the belief that God's kingdom comes on earth as individuals do his will through faith in Christ.

It is certainly *possible* to pray while walking in the country, or by the sea, or watching a rugger match. But it is something of a *tour de force*, and not remarkably appropriate. When we go to a rugger match on a Saturday afternoon or for a walk in the country, it is presumably God's will that we enjoy the match or the scenery, not that we pray. Relaxation, sport, and aesthetic pleasure are activities that are different from prayer, though it is admirable if they on some later occasion, or even there and then briefly, strike in the mind some transitory spark of thankfulness and praise.

One of the commonest questionable extensions of the idea of prayer is that to work is to pray. For this to be true the words must have slipped out of their usual meaning. The ultimate purpose of prayer is that we should know God and love him and do his will. Humanity has not been given any better explanation of being alive than this. When we are doing our daily work we are presumably doing the will of God; but we are not praying, and nothing is to be gained from saying that we are. This tendency to make everything 'mean' everything else is a common fault in the conversation of religious people. For example, in a discussion about liturgy sooner or later someone will say with intense earnestness, 'But liturgy is not a matter of ways of doing the Eucharist. Liturgy is *life*'. It is no help to clarity simply to get airborne in this way.

A similar difficulty is created by John Robinson's description,[1] 'Prayer is the responsibility to meet others with *all* I have . . . to expect to meet God in the way, not to turn aside from the way. All else is exercise towards that or reflection in depth upon it'. That is a good attempt at defining one of the ingredients of Christian love; it may well stand for that condition of self-disposal in which one hopes prayer will result, but it is not true to say that prayer *is* that. Prayer is in fact much nearer the 'all else' in that statement; it is, if not wholly, at any rate largely, 'exercise towards' such Christian disposal, sincerity, wholeness of living, and reflection in depth upon it.

Most of this exercise towards the Christian life is done in the

[1] J. Robinson, *Honest to God*, p. 100.

16

liturgy, in the public worship of the Church. Private prayer is an extension of this into one's seven attempts a week at living. The Lord's Prayer, the Confession, the Creed, the 'Lift up your hearts', and the 'Glory be to God on high' have been the principal points at which the liturgy has pressed through into the Christian's daily desire to sanctify time. Not much more is required. What needs to be added is some regular reflection on or remembrance of the principal events in the life of our Lord, some offering up to God of one's private joys and hates and griefs, and some moments of silent waiting in the presence, because there is too much talk in the world and so much of it is waste of time and breath, and the silent waiting of the religious mind is inexplicably fruitful. Five quiet minutes with the word 'God' in the centre of the mind, drawing our pitiful human thoughts and wants to the reality which that august word means in the Christian tradition, are five good minutes, and who knows how many more we are going to have? For the rest, it is the prayer of the community of Christian people that matters. And we immerse ourselves in this by participating in the public worship of the Church.

Of course, some people want to do more than this, they want to deepen their understanding of the Christian view of life, they want to become more familiar with its terms, its leading thoughts. When this happens, interest has been aroused and one does not have to drive oneself. The spiritual life is ruined for most people because it becomes dominated by a guilty conscience about religious duties. As long as prayer is something one feels one ought to do it remains a formidable bore. Probably people are well advised to do the minimum in private prayer until the hunger grows in them and they want to do more. Certainly the best way to quench the spirit is to burden people with daily Bible reading, daily prayers at length from devotional books, and long lists of people and causes to be prayed for as of obligation. It is better to start with the minimum and wait until one wants to do more, until one feels that there is more in the life of faith and that this more is sending some inviting signal to the mind.

The beginnings of prayer are present in most lives. Christian prayer consists of certain natural responses to life that have been trained to function within the life of faith and serve it. The most important of them are at the heart of the Eucharist, and they are thanking and offering. These motions of the mind have an infinite Christian significance, but they are human before they are Christian and they are just about as natural as breathing, though much more easily stifled.

Thankfulness is happiness spontaneously reaching out beyond itself, wanting to make contact with its cause. It is often easy to make this contact. The person responsible is there, in our presence, to be thanked. But often there is no identifiable cause, or it may be so multiple that we cannot encompass it in a single thought and we find ourselves simply saying 'Thank goodness'. When this natural response to life deepens, the entry into conscious religion becomes almost inevitable. Deep happiness reaches out to all the goodness there is, wanting to thank such ultimate goodness as is believed to make things occur as they do, bloom with so much light.

There is a point in happiness at which the mind simply rests in enjoyment, in a moment of tranquil attention to what is before it. The obvious examples are from the experience of what is beautiful—listening to music, looking at a painting, enjoying a landscape; and from the realm of simple relaxation—by the sea, watching the white crest of a wave falling down itself with a final shudder on to the wet sand while the mind relaxes, expands, reaches out to God knows what; and from the realm of love—the realization that you love and are loved and you search this mystery for words to hold it and finding none you know there is nothing to be done but silently rest in the centre of contentment. Most people may not observe themselves doing this, but this actually is the beginning of contemplation, the mind held still before some form or other of the goodness of life and simply glad to be in this presence. The great contemplatives have been people gifted with the ability to sustain this experience who developed it with mental and spiritual training.

Most of us cannot hold on to this stillness for long, though we may wish we could, and it is succeeded by the desire to make some expression of the joy that is in us; and this, when developed within Christian faith, becomes adoration.

In this way thanksgiving, contemplation and adoration are rooted in ordinary life. Every normal person again and again stands on the threshold of prayer.

The other part of the experience of prayer is offering. The

desire to serve or in some way propagate the goodness and beauty you have found in life, to be at its disposal and if possible a channel for it, may come to us only intermittently. But most people have some knowledge of the desire to give oneself, most commonly in the experience of love, but also in the realm of ordinary friendship, in professional or commercial loyalty, in devotion to a cause. This region of human wanting, wanting to give, provides more clues to the Christian idea of prayer and life than any other part of experience. And it is through it that the more difficult parts of prayer are best understood. These are confession, petition and intercession.

Confession is an offering of the self in the sense of a willingness to be known, a refusal to take refuge in concealment any more; it is a coming forward to present oneself 'just as I am' to be scrutinized by God and by oneself as well; it is a submission to the truth.

Petition and intercession, the asking for blessing for oneself and for others, create more problems than any other forms of prayer. They should always be closely related to the thought of offering. Our petitions and intercessions have themselves to be offered up to God. We must want to have these wishes placed in the whole structure of good which is God's will for the world. Even while putting these wants into words we relinquish our hold on the precise form we have given them, because we know that God's will may include or exclude the things we want. We are certain of course that we ourselves are wanted, as persons through whom some part of that congenial or uncongenial will is to be done. So we offer our wants and ourselves to God, ready for all this.

All prayer is some form or extension of thanking or offering. It is essentially something with which everyone is familiar. The purpose of Christian prayer is to deepen and intensify these human activities so that life is lived increasingly in thankful love.

2

Thanking

THE central and representative act of Christian prayer is known by five names, the Breaking of the Bread, the Lord's Supper, the Holy Communion, the Mass, the Eucharist. Each of these emphasizes a particular feature of the act, though oddly enough the most widely used title ('the Mass') has least meaning in itself and owes its powerful place in the Christian imagination entirely to that to which it refers.

The most satisfactory of the five is the word 'Eucharist'. This Greek word, meaning 'Thanksgiving', establishes the nature of the principal Christian act of prayer and also the quality of the essential Christian posture before experience. The Christian is a person whose mind is dominated by thankfulness. The believer who is a great sinner and yet preserves this characteristic element of thankfulness has still the essence of the kingdom of God within him. The upright and orthodox whose life is nevertheless more a wanting or a complaining than a thanking is in this respect not *recognizably* Christian, though formally he may be a member of the visible Church and is of course thereby part of it and shares fully in its privileges and responsibilities.

For most Christians in the world today the Eucharist, the Thanksgiving, is the main act of corporate prayer. One of its most solemn moments, the Sanctus, is preceded by the reminder how right it is, in the Christian view of things, to give thanks always and everywhere, whether life is sweet or sour. This is not just a matter of liturgical arrangement. It is a fact of Christian experience that thanksgiving and adoration are very closely bound together. If we have acquired, through various beneficent influences in our life, the readiness to enjoy and be thankful, we shall be next door to saying 'Holy, Holy, Holy'. We shall be on the edge of that awareness of the glory of God and the worthwhile-ness of life that is at the heart of Christian religion.

It is important for understanding the Christian way of life to cultivate the faculty of gratitude and nourish it as much as one can. The old evangelists used to work on our sense of unworthiness and sin and go on to argue that we therefore needed a saviour. This is not the theme for our time. The more a person of our time finds reasons for being thankful the more likely he is to come to belief in God in the Christian sense. And this is not at all easy. The images presented to the mind by the popular means of communication, television, radio, cinema, novel, the press, seem to be drawn with perverse persistence from the negative side of life, from the world of violence, destruction, guilt and death. A high price will be exacted from the society that allows this and encourages it. It can be criticized merely as a matter of mental hygiene. But the Christian believer has another reason for criticizing it, based on his conviction about what *is* right to do in any situation. What is right is that at all times and in all places we should give thanks.

It is Christian conviction that life in itself is neither meaningful nor holy, but that it can be made meaningful and holy. Thankfulness consecrates it, makes it meaningful and holy. Jesus and his friends were brought up in a world of thought in which to bless a thing and give thanks for it were one and the same. The idea is familiar in Christian tradition in grace before meals. The meal is blessed, that is to say, made holy, when God is thanked for it. Life is also blessed and made holy when it is received with thankfulness. It is not necessary that the thankfulness be always put into prayer or indeed into words at all. What matters is the thankfulness in the mind.

Life takes a lot of consecrating. Christians are inclined to think it a poor thing without Christ. But if it is lived thankfully it is well on the way to becoming a holy thing. Happiness almost of itself merges into holiness. There cannot be anything more worth working for than the happiness of men and women. This is why, as C. S. Lewis has pointed out,[1] the Psalms are so full of the idea of praise. It is because all happiness, 'all enjoyment spontaneously overflows into praise' ... 'the most balanced and capacious minds praise most, while the cranks, misfits and malcontents praise least'.

Christianity is a religion of happiness. It wants all men to be happy, to be able to live thankfully instead of resentfully. Resent-

[1] C. S. Lewis, *Reflections on the Psalms* (Fontana Edition), p. 80.

ul living is the alternative to thankful living, it is the condition of being against God and against life, unable to love either, and this is precisely the Christian idea of hell.

We cannot of course always live thankfully, though this is the Christian ideal. We need help with the dark side of life which always provokes resentment. Most people cannot understand how one could possibly be thankful for what one dislikes in life, how resentment could possibly become thankfulness. Part of the meaning of the Eucharist is that this extraordinary transfiguration of life is possible, but only when life is interpreted in terms of the whole event of Christ as the Church understands Christ. When life is so interpreted it becomes all thankfulness.

> 'And I heard every creature in heaven and on earth and under the earth and in the sea and all therein saying "To him who sits upon the throne and to the Lamb be blessing and honour and glory and might forever and ever!". And the four living creatures said "Amen!".'[1]

In this characteristic fragment of the Christian poetry the fulfilment of God's purpose is conceived by means of the image of a fantastic paean of praise from every creature that exists. Christian prayer centres round a thanksgiving for the fact that God has acted in Christ to free man from fear and self-concern and to release his pent-up power of loving. The pre-Christian past is seen in a kind of anticipatory glow shed on it by the Christ-event. And 'what the world is coming to' is similarly conceived in terms of praise.

But this ultimate praise and enthusiasm, this huge Amen— 'Amen' is a way of saying 'yes', it expresses the mind's joyful identification of itself with reality—all this is not something to look forward to, it is above time, it is that to which Christian worshippers are asked to 'lift up their hearts' in the Eucharist, it is one of the features of eternity. And in the Christian view eternity presses into time; when we live by the insights of faith, when we are 'in Christ', we are in fact in that eternal dimension and share, to some extent at any rate, its tremendous 'yes' to life. In the Eucharist we deliberately attempt to re-enter this dimension, to be drawn into Christ's magnificent, optimistic 'yes' to God and life. Christians believe that the attitude in which life is most fully

[1] Rev. v. 13.

understood and enjoyed is that of praise and thankfulness. This in the Christian view is always right, even when life seems on the surface to deserve nothing but one's hate or contempt. It may well be that in such extremity the Christian is reduced to seeing light nowhere but in the face of Christ, the one thank-worthy fact about life being that it contains his history and presence. But normally the rightness of being thankful should gradually dominate the Christian mind.

It will then excite gratitude for the presence of good wherever it is found, the good in nature, in the arts, in persons, and in the life of the community as produced by intelligent legislation and by scientific and industrial success. The Church seems to have a nose that is keener in scenting out evil than good. This is precisely the opposite of what Christian prayer should produce. If there are moral problems associated with twentieth-century affluence, with developments in education, in social medicine and in other fields of progress (as there certainly are), it is right that the Christian mind should be sensitive to them. But rejoicing in the good which these advances have produced would seem to be the more *characteristically* Christian response to life, and if the Church does not suggest this by its behaviour it is misinforming the world about Christianity.

This thankfulness extends beyond the area of recognizable good into that realm of perplexity in which we do not know how to place our labels 'good', 'bad'. It is felt to be right in any situation.

> When the believer thanks God for his creation, it seems to be a thanksgiving for his life as a whole, for everything, meaning the good *and* the evil within his life, since despite such evil, thanking God is still said to be possible. In devout religious believers, there seems to be no question of blaming God, but only of praising Him.[1]

It is this fact that is proclaimed every time the Church celebrates the Eucharist. It is unfortunate that familiarity with it reduces the essential strangeness of the Christian attitude to life. The Christian response to experience is unique in that through the Church flows a stream of thought which proclaims the rightness of thanking and adoring God at all times and everywhere, in peace and war, when you have lost all that you ever loved in this

[1] D. Z. Phillips, *The Concept of Prayer*, p. 97.

world, as well as when things are going as you desire. This attitude does not follow from contemplating the course of events as recorded in the press, the radio and television, but from contemplating the events reported by these means in the light of Christ, in the light of Christian faith as to what is the purpose of life for each individual who has to die eventually, and from faith as to how the whole enterprise of human life is going to be fulfilled.

Prayers of thanksgiving 'are the religious answer to the way things go, the recognition of the dependence of all things on God'.[1] When things go wrong for the believer, thanksgiving is still possible and right because he sees this wrongness in a wider and deeper context, within the infinitely hopeful understanding of life that the Church has received from Christ. In accepting this interpretation of life the believer has accepted the presence of pain in existence, the faith that evil can be turned to good and ultimately will be, the conviction that life is always and everywhere to be offered to God to be made part of the great work of turning evil into good which is his purpose, and the certainty that he is not being asked to endure his darkness alone. Accordingly, he sees more than the pain that is hurting him just now, and that 'more' is the whole pattern of thought implied in the word 'Christ'. This is why Christian praying always has Christ in the foreground of its thanking, with all the other goods of life set smaller around him. 'We bless thee for our creation, preservation and all the blessings of this life, but *above all* for thine inestimable love in the redemption of the world by our Lord Jesus Christ, for the means of grace, and for the hope of glory.'

It is far more important that young Christians should be taught that Christianity is a religion dominated by thankfulness than that 'he died to make us good'. This is not because goodness is unimportant but because Christianity interprets goodness in terms of love. The flow of love in us all is continually being stopped by self-preoccupation. Thankfulness and appreciation of life unlock the door of the prison of the self.

Until we are rescued from this prison, truth is denied us as well as love. We do not see the true nature of anything until, divested of self-concern, we attend to it, offer ourselves to it. In this attending and thankful self-offering we touch reality. Without them we must be insincere, functioning with only a part of our-

[1] Op. cit., p. 110.

selves. While we are immersed in our own thoughts we cannot recognize the reality of other people's needs, we do not see the other person at all as he is; all we see is a being who is or is not meeting our requirements. For this reason most domestic dissension is a battle between ghosts. Neither husband nor wife is loving or hating the real other, only an illusion, a projection of his or her personal wishes or resentments.

In this, and similar situations, exhortation to unselfishness is useless. But if the mind can learn to be quieter and silence the self-centred monologue and turn its full attention to the being of another person, knowing and loving can grow out of that. This difficulty in seeing the reality of another person because one's own mind is a fog of lonely yearning and rage is a characteristic twentieth-century problem, and one, incidentally, which figures largely in the drama, novel, cinema of our time. If I have to impress others for the sake of raising my own self-respect, or blame them because I cannot assume responsibility for myself, or defeat them because of my need to triumph somehow, somewhere, one thing is clear—that I shall never see them as they are. For this reason love itself in our civilization has a great struggle to be genuine.

Thanking, adoring and contemplating are the primary acts in the Christian use of praying, because in the Christian understanding of experience there is so much to praise and love, and because the more the self is turned to the not-self in communion the more it becomes itself as created by God instead of the self-made distortion of this we carry around most of the time. The more the real self is freed from what we *think* it is or feel it *ought* to be and is allowed to be the alive centre of our existence, the more we can treat other people with a similar relaxation and generosity. We stop wanting them to measure up to our requirements, we are able to accept them as they are, we find that there is room in our thoughts for other beings, as alive and awkward and needy as ourselves. This is to walk out of the self into the real world, the only world in which genuine love is possible.

3

Adoring and Contemplating

IN the Christian use of praying it is understood that we can address God in personal terms, calling him 'Father' in the surprisingly intimate way that was a feature of the prayer of Jesus. The word 'Abba' which he used is sometimes expounded as the equivalent of the word 'Daddy'. In a sense this is true but the fact that it immediately sets up an embarrassment within us shows that such exposition will not function helpfully for us today. But the peculiarly, even intensely, personal way in which Jesus addressed God is part of the truth about Christ.

Christian prayer is addressed to God as the Church understands him. It is addressed to the Holy Trinity, the complex mystery that the word 'God' means for Christians, though it would be more accurate to say that the Christian prays *to* the fatherhood believed by Jesus to be the principal characteristic of God's being, *through* the son—through all that Jesus taught us about God, and *in* the power, fellowship and instruction of the spirit which animates the community of faith and is in some degree within the mind of every praying Christian. The awkwardness and complexity of this way of thinking about Christian prayer at any rate does justice to the mystery of faith and saves it from becoming naïve and magical.

But this trinitarian being is always addressed in personal terms. God, for the Christian, is a Thou, not an It.

This does not mean that God is *a person*. The personal address is used because to think of God in a personal category saves us from regarding him as a remote, intellectual abstraction—to be understood if we have the brains for such matters but not to be worried about if we have not succeeded in achieving any 'O' levels. The personal address is the only medium for registering the fact of his accessibility, his unpredictable aliveness, that he might speak even to me, that I can answer but cannot use him.

Sometimes Christians have been apologetic about this aspect of their religion, but quite unnecessarily.

> The kinds of conduct which are primary to Christian faith—praying, hearing, confession of sin, repentance, gratitude, hope, love—are ones that belong to the relation of Thou to Thou and as such are all of them naïve, but they are neither primitive nor mythical, and have therefore no need to fear reflection.[1]

> Christian faith is the courage to consider the world's mystery of the power on which we are absolutely dependent to the last depths of our being and interpret it in the light of the encounter with a Thou. The anthropomorphic character of Christian talk of God accordingly does not mean a limitation which we must strive to overcome, but is a sign of the exaltedness of the thought of revelation founded on the person of Jesus.[2]

What we need to remember when we use these terms is that their meaning is determined by God as he has revealed himself and continues to reveal himself in the Christian Church, not by our experience of their human reference. The 'fatherhood of God' is indicated by his dealings with humanity in the light of the Christ-event, not by a human father's relationship with his children, though this in fact indicates the line along which we can fruitfully think about God, as long as we are prepared for modifications of a quite drastic nature when we apply this human situation to the being and action of God.

> Personal terms like father and son, mother and child, lord and servant, friendship and the like, become applicable to our relation to him, but he is not subjected to them, i.e. the reference to him determines the application. In what sense he is Father, Lord, Friend, etc., and how far these expressions are valid of him, can be ascertained only in view of his actions, not beforehand. . . . But in bestowing himself as Father, Lord, etc., he reserves to himself the way in which he actualizes the relations thereby indicated. All our words must be 'given a bath' says Luther—to be still more precise: they must go through the cross. For it is at the cross of Jesus that his disciples and with them the Church must first learn how sovereignty, the kingdom, the love, the righteousness of God are actualized.[3]

[1] H. Gollwitzer, *The Existence of God*, p. 159.
[2] P. Althaus, quoted in Gollwitzer, op. cit., p. 200, n. 2.
[3] H. Gollwitzer, *The Existence of God*, pp. 163-4.

The Christian, living his faith, interprets life not in terms of his personal reaction to it but of what he believes God is doing in it and with it. He understands life as a flow of happenings that cannot be separated from God and therefore is only rightly spoken *to*, not *of*, 'in verbs and in the form of doxology, in adoration and glorification'[1] of its Creator and Sustainer.

At the same time the personal category withdraws God from our familiarity and domination. Persons are centres of freedom and endless surprise. Even the person, whom after years of companionship and love we think we know, can surprise, disappoint and shock us. In human life a person can never be fully *understood* but can be fully *loved*, loved to the limit of the lover's capacity to love. This is the principal justification for using the idea of 'love' of God; it is why one of the greatest of Christian mystics said of God 'by love he can be caught and held, but by thinking never'.[2]

But if 'love' is the right word, the dominant word, in the Christian religion, there must inevitably be an interest in and search for and love of God in himself. Normally the person who loves is concerned more with whom or what he loves than with the satisfactions left in the mind as a result of loving. He wishes to know, be with, be united to what he loves.

And this is what the Christian is seeking in adoration. He has gone beyond thanking. He is praising and wanting that which he dimly discerns as the ultimate cause, value, giver in all his experience of the joy of life and of the productiveness of painful life. He can express this longing only in personal terms, he has the example of Jesus for the legitimacy of doing this, and he finds that, when he expresses his longing in personal terms, the reality he desires becomes increasingly personal to him, though he knows that God is infinitely more than personal. 'He speaks as "I" when we truly call him "Thou".'[3]

Adoration is a rejoicing in what we believe God is in himself, in the more that he must be that we cannot understand; it is a reaching out to this in love and longing, wanting to know and prove as much of this as is permitted here on earth, going to that rim of experience where something tells you to turn back to life

[1] Op. cit., p. 212.
[2] *The Cloud of Unknowing* (Penguin Edition), p. 60.
[3] C. S. Lewis, *Letters to Malcolm* (Fontana Edition), p. 23.

because this is as far as you can go in wonder at the devastating richness of life. The rest we may hope to know after death, but it is not for now.

It is possible to be so impressed with this part of the life of prayer that we give it priority. This is certainly not a Methodist problem. The prayer of the Methodist fellowship-group or prayer meeting is so preoccupied with intercession that thanking and adoring hardly find a place, though they are exactly the antidote to our self-consciousness and activism. But in other traditions it has been argued that the only authentic Christian prayer is adoration. This is a very attractive exaggeration, and forgivable because it is such a true anticipation of the end of life, but it cannot be true of our life on earth.

Whilst we are living earthly life, the true prayer, the basic Christian posture is eucharist, it is the giving of thanks. It is thanks for natural life and supernatural life, it is thanks for the birth we had of our parents and the re-birth we have had in Christ. Thanksgiving is not adoration. It is next door to adoration. And in the Eucharist the next action after the affirmation that at all times and in all places we should give thanks is the Adoration, the Sanctus itself. And this is a kind of allegory.

There is something not absolutely final about thanksgiving. To be thankful leads to something else, to work, to appropriate action. The more thankful I am for my education the more I want educational prospects for everyone improved. The more thankful I am for my Christian understanding of life, inadequate as it is and full of mistakes, the more I want to serve the Church.

On the other hand there is indeed something final about praise and adoration. One can rest there, one wants to rest there. There is nothing to come after, just as there is nothing to come after the applause as the curtain comes down on the last act of a great play. There is nothing to do after ultimate praise. Adoration is literally the end. And that is why it is only a transitory phenomenon in this world. It is really out of its element in time. All earthly adoration is an anticipation, legitimate or illegitimate, of eternity.

This is the essence of the temptation of beauty. The aesthete wants nothing but to enjoy and adore. He is wanting what in the Christian view is never fully to be given us here, the life of heaven on earth.

The great romantics seem to have understood this. It would be difficult to find a more characteristically romantic work than Wagner's *Tristan and Isolde*. That work concludes with one of the most beautiful statements ever made of the idea that in the world of time there is nothing that can possibly follow the full vision of beauty and love except death.

The Christian view is that for this life the word is eucharist, thankfulness, and what follows from that—love, service, pain, struggle, crucifixion. For the next life, for the realm of consummation, all our earthly concepts are of course useless, but Christians have persistently thought of the ultimate kingdom in terms of adoration, an endless sanctus.

The Christian who prays is trying to feed that life of faith in which he trusts he will see more clearly what it means to love God and his neighbour and will increasingly have the strength and insight to put this idea of love into practice.

Prayer is therefore a means to loving. It is repeatedly said by the great spiritual directors that the test of the value of one's prayer is the kind of life one lives when one is not formally praying.

William Temple is often quoted as saying 'the proper relation in thought between prayer and conduct is not that conduct is supremely important and prayer may help it, but that prayer is supremely important and conduct tests it'.[1] This is one of those characteristically true sayings about the Christian way of life that cannot stand alone without some qualification.

It is true that our life shows what is going on in the inner world of desire from which authentic prayer rises. It is true that the desire for God himself, in himself, for the face that is behind all the faces of love and haunts them all, even the most beautiful, with the tantalization and summons of penultimacy, is never going to be taken from any of us. Christians believe that it is the one aspiration that is ultimately going to grasp its object with some fantastic sob of recognition and that it is completely misunderstood when it is regarded as 'a means towards the moral virtues and the works of the active life'[2] in this world.

But here and now we live in penultimacy, in temporality. We cannot seize wholly now on that which we believe will be given us in the final then. And for here and now St. John of the Cross has

[1] William Temple, *Christus Veritas*, p. 45.
[2] J. Maritain, *Prayer and Intelligence*, p. 32.

given us a more penetrating saying: 'At eventide they will examine thee in love.'[1] It would seem then that beginners in the Christian life will find it helpful to think that love is the important thing and that prayer feeds it. Certainly if prayer does not feed love it is hard to justify it. The prayer that is prayer for its own sake, contemplation that enjoys its solitary communing with the ultimate but does not issue in love, seems like some absurd attempt to get out of time into eternity. This is really religious self-indulgence. Julien Green said: 'L'âme est sensuelle à sa manière.'[2]

It is true that the saints had moments of great joy in prayer, and these they took as earnests of the richer union with God that will be possible when we have finished with life in time and space. But, apart from saying 'Eye hath not seen nor ear heard neither have entered into the heart of man the things which God hath prepared for them that love him,'[3] what can we say about heaven except that we long for it and do not know what we precisely long for when we long for it? The new testament idea of heaven contains the thought of an absolute and ultimate praise, under the image of the adoration of the Lamb.

Thanking is the characteristic Christian state. It leads naturally to adoration, to the desire to praise the cause of our joy, not for having caused our joy (the self and its satisfactions have been by now left behind) but for what he is and must be in himself. This can become so persistent and excited that we begin to want a union with God and knowledge of him which it is not legitimate to expect in this life and, as far as we can see, is not going to be given us. 'My soul thirsts for God, for the living God. When shall I come and behold the face of God?'[4]

But there is a point in this process of praise at which the mind finds it possible simply to rest in contentment with one or other of the forms of God's presence that are in fact given us in this world. This affectionate looking at and resting in appreciated good is contemplation. Much of the experience cannot be put into words; indeed it seems to be part of the experience that verbalization is effectively stopped; but it contains the conviction that this

---

[1] *St. John of the Cross* (ed. E. A. Peers), vol. 3, p. 247.
[2] Julien Green, *Journal*, vol. 4, p. 38.
[3] 1 Cor. ii, 9. (A.V.)
[4] Psalm 42. 2.

segment of reality in front of me has an infinite value, that beside it I myself do not matter at all, yet in being in its presence and loving it I seem to be at home, more myself, more alive than I am elsewhere; I know that it is good to be here and that it is a pity that life is not always like this; it is a kind of accusation against life that this must end and I return to what with devastating precision is called 'ordinary life'.

This experience is far more common than is commonly acknowledged. It is certainly not the preserve of those who are called mystics. Some of it is part of the regular experience of human beings, whatever their faith, degree of Christian faith, inability consciously to adhere to any faith.

> Wherever a man's mind has been uplifted, his temptations thwarted, his sorrows comforted, his resolutions strengthened, his aberrations controlled, by the sight of purity, innocence, love or beauty—indeed, wherever he has, even for a moment, recognized and responded to the distinction between good and evil, between better and worse,—such a man has had in part the mystical experience. Dim though his mirror may have been, he has yet seen God. Where he has seen God once there he may see him again. . . . So far then from being rare, the mystical experience is at once the commonest and greatest of human accidents. There is not one of us to whom it does not come daily. It is only carelessness or custom that prevents our realizing how divine it is in essence; only timidity which checks us from proclaiming that we too at such moments have seen God, even if as in a glass darkly. . . . What Christianity offers, with its fellowship and sacraments, its life of prayer and service, its preaching of the Incarnate Son of God, is the same vision in ever-increasing plenitude.[1]

This does not mean that the Christian thinks that practically everyone is 'working with some kind of concept of God under other names and therefore already stands in a much more positive relation to the God of Christian faith than he himself is aware'.[2] But it does mean that there are, as Simone Weil puts it, implicit forms of the love of God in most lives and these can act as sympathetic leads to the Christian's more articulate and dynamic love of God. She says, for example, that the sense of beauty 'is present in all the preoccupations of secular life. If it

---

[1] K. E. Kirk, *The Vision of God* (abridged edition), pp. 193–4.
[2] H. Gollwitzer, *The Existence of God*, p. 245.

were made true and pure it would sweep all secular life in a body to the feet of God'.[1] She points out that there is an incompleteness and pain about aesthetic love because its object is things which are incapable of answering to man's love, incapable of saying 'yes', of surrendering. Ultimately we long to love the beauty of the world in the form of a living, responding being; and this is essentially the longing for the Incarnation.[2] St. Augustine, in his *Confessions*, makes the similar point that all are seeking God but settle unsatisfactorily and unsatisfyingly for that which is less than God; and in the *De Trinitate* he says 'Souls in their very sins seek but a sort of likeness of God'.[3]

But in these experiences of heightened awareness of life it is possible to rest in contentment. Normally the mind functions by means of sense-impressions, images (that is to say thoughts of a pictorial nature), and ideas (thoughts of an abstract, conceptual nature). But the mind can function in another way. In the experience of the arts (listening to music, looking at a picture), or when enjoying the view of a wide and various landscape, or in certain moments of tranquillity and happiness in the infinitely diverse experience of human love, the mind seems not to be doing anything at all; it is certainly not pursuing a series of verbal thoughts, it is simply attending in quietness and joy to what is in front of it. It is this faculty of the mind to attend, without one thought giving way to another, simply to be held, that is the characteristic feature of contemplation. Practically everyone is familiar with it. It is the commonest, wisest, safest way into God. The mystics of the great religions were people who were specially gifted with this mental aptitude and cultivated it according to their understanding of God.

What this type of experience means can, of course, be variously interpreted, but Christian spirituality has usually wanted to refer it to God.

> During the contemplation of a work of art, or while listening to a melody, the effort to understand relaxes, and the soul simply delights itself in the beauty which it divines . . . or merely a memory, a word, a line of Dante or Racine, shooting up from the obscure depths of our soul, seizes hold of us, recollects and pene-

[1] Simone Weil, *Waiting on God* (Kegan Paul), p. 101.
[2] Simone Weil, *Waiting on God* (Kegan Paul). p. 108.
[3] St. Augustine, *Confessions* (Everyman edition), pp. 26-9, and p. 29 footnote.

C   33

trates us. After this experience we know no more than we did, but we have the impression of understanding a little something that before we hardly knew, of tasting a fruit at the rind of which we have scarcely nibbled.[1]

A more recent writer argues more tentatively for this experience but eventually comes to make a similar claim for it:

> The conclusion to which I came at this point is that this peculiarly intense activity of mind . . . is of the greatest value because it makes us aware of *ourselves* as we never are in other circumstances. . . . We really 'come alive', as we might put it. It is not merely that we are enjoying ourselves enormously. . . . We find ourselves transported into a mysterious region of *value*, and at the same time it is a sort of home-coming or an intimation, of a peculiarly dynamic or (it may be) even of an overwhelming kind, that there is a goal which seems to recede even as we approach it.[2]

But it is an earlier writer, oddly enough, the poet Baudelaire, who speaks most confidently for the religious interpretation of this experience:

> It is at once by poetry and by penetrating beyond it, by music and by penetrating beyond it, that the soul catches a glimpse of the splendour on the other side of the grave; and when an exquisite poem brings tears to the eyes, these tears are no proof of excessive pleasure. They are, rather, the witness of an irritated sensibility, a demand of the nerves, of a nature exiled in the imperfect, which longs to *seize immediately* on this very earth the paradise revealed to it.[3]

These experiences may not always be interpreted in such visionary terms, but it is our faith that they are the presence of God, from the momentary thrills of joy in life and love of it that come to us all to the sustained stillness of tranquil love attained by the disciplined contemplative. No one doubts that they are times of infinitely important living and that we are fools not to explore them more—to understand them better and to prepare the mind for their more frequent visitation. It is clear that they are always *given*. We do not make them ourselves. They come gratuitously and often unexpectedly. But it seems that a loving openness to

---

[1] De Grandmaison, quoted in H. Brémond, *Prayer and Poetry*, p. 89.
[2] Dom Illtyd Trethowan, *Theology and the University* (ed. Coulson), p. 196.
[3] Charles Baudelaire, *Les Fleurs du Mal* (ed. Starkie), p. xiii.

experience and the ability to wait in silence make us more susceptible to them. It is possible to prolong their presence by resting in such experience thankfully while it is there, letting the beauty of the moment work its work on us instead of rushing on to the next bit of ambiguous experience of twentieth-century life. And this may well increase our responsiveness to the approach of these moments. And there is much evidence that, if cultivated, their influence spreads an enlightenment over the rest of life. Indeed action is inseparably connected with contemplation in the Christian use of praying; it is not an interruption of it but an addition to it, as Aquinas said,[1] making a perfect whole of two elements which, singly, are incomplete and need each other.

'In the beginning was the Word, this is he to whom Mary listened; and the Word was made Flesh, this is he whom Martha served.'[2] Christian life is a life of listening and serving, waiting on God and loving him in his creation, and the serving and the loving are purified and directed by the listening and waiting. Waiting, listening, and silence are not the twentieth-century Christian's strong suit. But knowledge of both the truth of life and one's real self arise from them and the detachment they involve. And our need of them is increasingly realized.

'I have a feeling,' I said, 'about the axial lines of life, with respect to which you must be straight or else your existence is merely clownery, hiding tragedy. I must have had a feeling since I was a kid about these axial lines which made me want to have my existence on them, and so I have said "no" like a stubborn fellow to all my persuaders, just on the obstinacy of my memory of these lines, never entirely clear. But lately I have felt these thrilling lines again. When striving stops, there they are as a gift. I was lying on the couch here before and they suddenly went quivering right straight through me. Truth, love, peace, bounty, usefulness, harmony! And all noise and grates, distortion, chatter, distraction, effort, superfluity, passed off like something unreal. And I believe that any man at any time can come back to these axial lines, even if an unfortunate bastard, if he will be quiet and wait it out. . . .'[3]

Contemplative prayer used to be regarded as a level of prayer

---

[1] Cf. Jacques Maritain, *Prayer and Intelligence*, pp. 18–19. This little book is a valuable summary of Thomistic teaching on prayer.

[2] St. Augustine, quoted in Jacques Maritain, op. cit., p. 31.

[3] Saul Bellow, *The Adventures of Augie March* (Penguin Edition), p. 524

to be reached only by people of great sanctity, by people living in religious communities, or by people who have this particular gift. It is no longer thought that this kind of prayer is to be so restricted. It is in fact open to all who are capable of thankfulness, appreciation of life, and love of the world of persons and things. Indeed the ordinary Christian is much more likely to pray rightly in this form than when he is interceding, which has for some time been (mistakenly) the most natural form of Christian prayer. Contemplation is the way in to prayer for most people in our generation. They should begin here, by being thankful, by being attentive to the experience they enjoy, by endeavouring to hold themselves quietly and appreciatively in the presence of the good which is pleasing them, and by holding themselves there as long as they can.

Words play very little part in this prayer. It can rightly conclude with some act of praise, but its main feature is that it is loving and looking, not discursive thinking. It is true that it is often the outcome of 'prayerful pondering' of some passage of scripture.[1] But the prayer itself is in the main a wordless attention to some experienced or considered segment of the goodness of life. In the ordinary experience of daily life it must necessarily be a fleeting attention and thankfulness.

But it is worth while attempting to cultivate this attitude. It cannot be done without quiet and solitude. Even in our time of noise and activity it is possible occasionally (perhaps once a week) to use a quarter or half an hour in lunch time or at the end of the day's work for being quiet in the presence of God. The growing use of Retreats is a sign of people's increasing desire for the quiet and solitude in which this kind of prayer can best be learned.

It can, however, be practised without these aids. It is possible to make a simple act of faith in the presence of God and continue what one is doing in that faith. There is the use of the 'Jesus Prayer' which we shall consider later.[2] There is the cultivation of awareness of the 'sacrament of the present moment'.[3] A visit to a museum or art gallery, the reading of a classical author, or going

---

[1] Cf. De Caussade, *On Prayer*, Dialogue 5, p. 197.
[2] Archbishop Anthony Bloom, *Living Prayer*, chs. 6 and 8.
[3] This is discussed in Chapter 11.

to the theatre where a play from the past is being performed—
these activities give one a sense of relatedness to the past, some
awareness of *a* communion of saints, if not the specifically Christian understanding of that phrase. Similarly, walking in the
countryside or cultivating our back garden can maintain our
awareness of the natural world and our participation in that
creatureliness that is full of the throb of life and the threat of
death. These activities can provoke some sense of the continuity
of life and of the glory of God in creation and providence, and
accordingly become sources of thankfulness and joy at the way
life is arranged.

There is a very useful pamphlet by John Townroe[1] which ably
expounds some of the forms of contemplative prayer particularly
suited to life in our time, a time in which people find it difficult to
find time even for love, never mind prayer, though the two are
more closely connected than is sometimes realized. For the times
when we can give ourselves unreservedly to prayer there is much
help to be derived from Dom John Chapman's essay *Contemplative Prayer: a few simple rules*,[2] and from the teaching of De
Caussade to whom Chapman was greatly indebted.[3]

As a matter of fact, after reading De Caussade's *Abandonment to
Divine Providence* and the English work, whose author is unknown,
called *The Cloud of Unknowing*, one feels that there is not very much
more to be said about private prayer. There is also a peculiar
sense that this area of Christian experience is one in which dialogue between east and west could easily begin. Indeed, when a
believer who has any familiarity with the Christian tradition of
ascetic theology reads the Yoga Sutras of Patanjali[4] he has a
peculiar sense, if not of having been here before, of being in no
strange land. If he continues reading and thinking in this Hindu
tradition he may well come to the conclusion that Christian
prayer is theologically to be preferred, in that the doctrine of the
Incarnation keeps Christian love consistently directed to people
rather than things or concepts (even of the divine nature), lovely
as some things are, attractive as some thoughts of God are, hateful

---

[1] John Townroe, *Prayer for busy people* (publ. S.P.C.K.).
[2] John Chapman, *Spiritual Letters*, p. 287.
[3] De Caussade, *Abandonment to Divine Providence*; and *On Prayer*, pp. 266–73.
[4] Cf. Ernest Wood, *Yoga*; Geraldine Coster, *Yoga and the Western Psychology*.

as some people are, but that Patanjali is certainly superior to the Christian tradition on the psychosomatic aspect of prayer, on the place and character of physical discipline in the cultivation of mental detachment and control.

4

Confessing

ST. Luke records a story which, he says, Jesus told in order that
we should persevere in prayer and not despair.[1] It is about a
woman who repeatedly asks a judge to vindicate her against
someone who has wronged her, and eventually succeeds. Jesus's
comment on this story is that God will similarly vindicate his
chosen. This idea, that God will at last show his hand and confirm
the faith of those who believe that life has the meaning the Bible
gives to it, and confound the hostility or indifference of those who
do not believe such things, is one of the traditional Bible ways of
thinking about the final completion of God's purpose for
humanity. If St. Luke is right in thinking that the story concerns
prayer, that is what the praying is about—the meaning and
fulfilment of life.

So Jesus is not thinking of the problem of persevering at such
rule of prayer as one may have adopted. It is in fact hard to keep
such a rule going, but that is not the point here. He is thinking of
our longing for a time when all the doubt and uncertainty is over
and it is as clear as the day that we were right all along and the
others were wrong.

This longing was part of the outlook Jesus inherited as a Jew. It
is of course an unsatisfactory way of thinking; one suspects here
that it is already disintegrating for him, that he wants to put it all
very differently. New thoughts are already taking shape in his
mind.

'And will not God vindicate his elect who cry to him day and
night?... I tell you, he will vindicate them speedily. Nevertheless,
when the Son of man comes, will he find faith on earth?'[1] That
is to say, if you ask whether we are ever going to enjoy something more than faith, ever going to see face to face and know
even as we have been known in a knowledge that is final and infinitely satisfying, the Christian answer is 'Yes, that is in fact the

---

[1] Luke xviii. 1–8. [2] Luke xviii. 7–8 (R.S.V.).

39

promise; the promise is that God will in fact show that he is, and that he is what in Jesus Christ he has declared himself to be'.

Faith is to live continually, perseveringly within that promise. It awakens joy and longing and fear in us. But faith is to keep living within it. But how many people do really live in that mental world, that kind of faith?

And that is where Jesus breaks it up—with his characteristic 'Yes, but . . .', so that we think we have been comforted a little and then it does not look like that at all, and we are left wondering whether we know much at all about faith, certainly doubting whether we ourselves will qualify for that moment when certainty is given and God proves himself.

St. Luke follows with this famous paragraph:

> He also told this parable to some who trusted in themselves that they were righteous and despised others: 'Two men went up into the temple to pray, one a Pharisee and the other a tax collector. The Pharisee stood and prayed thus with himself, "God, I thank thee that I am not like other men, extortioners, unjust, adulterers, or even like this tax collector. I fast twice a week, I give tithes of all I get." But the tax collector, standing far off, would not even lift up his eyes to heaven, but beat his breast, saying, "God, be merciful to me a sinner!" I tell you, this man went down to his house justified rather than the other; for every one who exalts himself will be humbled, but he who humbles himself will be exalted.'[1]

In these verses we are given some of Jesus's thoughts about the kind of faith that in his view is in fact faith, the faith which will ultimately become sight.

It is a faith which no longer thinks in terms of an adversary who is to be put clearly in the wrong, into the shadow cast by our right. This is what the woman in the first story wants—personal vindication. This is what the pharisee in the second story is using his religion for—to keep in with God and establish his personal superiority over less religious or non-religious men. So also the Christian today who wants the arguments of the humanist proved wrong, and the social impact of the Church clearly seen, and the world agreeing that Christianity is relevant to our time, so that he himself can feel the ground a little firmer under his feet, is really wanting one or another of the various kinds of justification. He desires some form of being proved to be right.

[1] Luke xviii. 9–14 (R.S.V.).

But Christianity can never provide this. The non-believing world is not our adversary. It and we stand together under the mercy and judgement of God. If for our being right it is necessary for the humanist to be shown to be wrong, that is not the kind of faith to which the Son of God will reveal himself.

The faith that is Christian is the faith that looks round at life and sees no adversaries, has no grievances, makes no claims, but simply wants to be in relationship and to love.

St. Luke says the pharisee prayed with himself, which is to say he did not pray at all. He is an unrelated being talking to himself in the monologue of justification. If we desire to be right we shall end by being alone. It is true that there is much that is hateful about life and that many mistakes are made that do not seem to involve us in any serious self-scrutiny. But there is a deeper understanding of the human condition than this.

There is a kind of faith which is certain that we are all bound up in the human situation together, sharing guilt and obligations in ways too subtle to be sorted out now. The general background of the moral life for any sensitive person must be a vague sense of the goodness and wrongness of life and that we are all involved. In the foreground are the more personal items of joy and guilt each of us has to be thankful and perturbed about. It is not possible to do anything but stand in this situation and accept it in faith—in the faith that there is a divine mercy that will have mercy upon us to the end and at the end, in that mercy of which we have had many hints so far. We do not *know* that he will have mercy upon us; we are not sure that we are justified in so believing. The point of this crucial passage in the New Testament wisdom is that justification, being in the right, is not really on, at any rate the *feel* of it. It is possible, of course, that you may walk down to your house weeping all the way and yet, unknown to yourself, be justified—but that is because what is in fact 'on' is faith and humility. For these, according to Jesus, there seems to be a future. The road of life goes through them.

Prayers of confession are the outcome of this kind of faith and humility, this abandonment of the desire to be right. It requires a certain security. The more insecure we feel the more we are driven to justify ourselves somehow. Accordingly, penitence can never spring from the realization of one's sins. The evangelists who used to attempt to awaken the sense of sin by describing our abysmal moral failure did not understand the Christian religion. The sense of sin cannot come from self-hatred or fear.

On the contrary, it is the result of adoration. It flows naturally out of the security that comes into one's life as one is led to a positive view of the goodness of life and the glory and love of God. It flowers and fruits only in fertile stretches of happiness. If any one had the luck really to see life as a welcoming love he would begin to feel nervous and ashamed about what his current attempt at being human amounted to. This nervous hesitation and its gentle but inexorable defeat is set out perfectly in George Herbert's poem 'Love bade me welcome: yet my soul drew back'. It is marvellous how much Christianity goes into so small a space.

> Love bade me welcome: yet my soul drew back,
>   Guilty of dust and sin.
> But quick-eyed Love, observing me grow slack
>   From my first entrance in,
> Drew nearer to me, sweetly questioning
>   If I lacked anything.
> 'A guest', I answered, 'worthy to be here':
>   Love said, 'You shall be he'.
> 'I the unkind, the ungrateful? Ah, my dear,
>   I cannot look on thee'.
> Love took my hand, and smiling did reply.
>   'Who made the eyes but I?'
> 'Truth Lord, but I have marred them: let my shame
>   Go where it doth deserve'.
> 'And know you not', says Love, 'who bore the blame?'
>   'My dear, then I will serve'.
> 'You must sit down', says Love, 'and taste my meat'.
>   So I did sit and eat.

The sudden recognition of the mystery of goodness and holiness in life as a whole, or gathered intensely in some representative being, may well draw from the astonished heart something like Peter's 'Depart from me for I am a sinful man, O Lord!'. But normally the process is gradual. As your conviction that God is love, that life is good, increases, automatically your defences crumble, you wish to be occupied more in loving life than in protecting your self and shoring up its pretensions. Trust becomes stronger than recoil, and you find yourself willing to be exposed to at any rate much more of the truth than you ever thought you could endure. Finally, from the depths of the self, there rises the desire to offer one's life to the truth, ready to see what that light candidly shows.

At any time, of course, this process can be reversed. One can become defensive again, chasing after justifications and superiorities, decking a phoney self in them. Always when things go wrong this is likely to happen. Unhappiness always drives us into unreality. The happier you are the more your soul can bear to be shown the depth of inbred sin.

As it naturally derives from thankfulness and adoration, confession should return into thankfulness as soon as possible. The mind cannot take the truth about itself without the truth about God. Far more people 'live in sin' than realize it. The sense of sin is a rotten bit of life to stay in for long, and one should fairly quickly look round for the exit. The exit is forgiveness, and the resolve now to look at more attractive realities that lead the mind hopefully away from yesterday.

When we confess our sins we are not telling God anything he does not know. He was with us and obscurely in us when we were doing the sins we are confessing. As Christians, we drag Christ into all our hates and indulgences. It is impossible to inform God. The central and representative act of Christian prayer, the Eucharist, in the Anglican and Methodist rite, chooses this aspect of God as its starting point—that whatever we are doing in the ensuing hour we certainly do not think we are telling God anything, because he knows all there is to know about humanity, even the most secret pains and desires hidden away in the labyrinth of our minds.

We confess in order to express our acceptance of this fact, our willingness to be so known, and our desire to enter as far as we can into this searching knowledge God has of us. We stop the life of concealment, of pretending that no one knows or need know. We say we know we are living in the light, we are content to have it so, only more so, we want to be wholly in the light if possible. It is not wholly possible subjectively, because we cannot bear the whole truth, but confession is the desire for as much as we can bear.

Mr. John Wain, explaining his position as a writer, says: 'To write well . . . is a matter of feeling and living at the required depth, fending off the continual temptation to be glib and shallow . . . to be evasive and shirk the hard issues. It is a matter of training oneself to live with reality, and, as our greatest living poet has warned us: "Human kind cannot bear very much reality". But, if one is to write well, one *must* bear it: increasing the dose, perhaps, until one can absorb it in quantities that would unhinge the ordinary person.'[1] It is this desire for reality that makes a person risk the prayer of confession.

The deeper this desire the stronger will be the conviction that what this prayer intends cannot be fully done without the use of sacramental confession. There is a vagueness about private confession to God. The desire for spiritual progress sags into the mediocrity of a general wish to be somehow better. It would seem to sail smoothly on the assumption that one knows all about the will of God and its relation to the self, that one also knows one's self as thoroughly as a brief shopping list, whereas both God and self are mysteries we can do little more than begin to enter. Our sins spring from fears and resentments whose roots are mostly obscure to us. We continually need help to see and understand ourselves if we want to see and understand. The Russian theologian Alexis Khomiakov wrote: 'We know that when anyone falls he falls alone; but no one is saved alone. He is saved in the Church, as a member of it.' In sacramental confession we offer ourselves to the God of truth and the truth of God as members of the Church and within its ordered life. We know that God knows us through and through but we make an act of acceptance of this, of willingness to be known just as we discreditably are, and we do it through a particular means of grace the Church has traditionally provided for this. 'Instead of merely being known, we show, we tell, we offer ourselves to view.'[2]

The *Confiteor* of the Mass expresses this 'being offered to view' with a marvellous adequacy. It shows that the act of confession is the sinner's refusal to be alone,[3] his realization that his sins were always open affairs, in God's presence and that of the Church triumphant. He is willing to say that this is the truth about them, and he is ready to take responsibility for them, but not alone—he wants to appeal to these who *know*, the host of heaven, and this earthly priest who is with him representatively of the whole Body, to help him in this risky adventure of honesty.

[1] John Wain, *Sprightly Running*, p. 263 (1962).
[2] C. S. Lewis, *Letters to Malcolm*, p. 22 (Fontana Books).
[3] Jacques Rivière, *À La Trace De Dieu*, pp. 196-9.

Confessing

And he needs all this help. The Christian who attempts to reach his personal truth has undertaken a formidable task.[1] Through fear we tend to rate ourselves higher than the reality we suspect. But the hunger for truth cannot be met by such insubstantial fare. Suppose we dare to go forward a short way into the self. We do not take long to meet despair, to encounter the gloom that descends when we are disillusioned about ourselves or when we realize that our cruelties or indulgences have consequences we are afraid to live through. The mind has to be *led* to the truth, *encouraged* to reject illusion and avoid despair, and *be assured* of the forgiving presence of God. And then it is a question of whether that assurance can hold the mind long enough for adoration and trust to form again, because only then one can live with this new knowledge of oneself and, with confidence and hope, work through such results of one's mistakes as remain to be worked through.

One of the facts of the spiritual life which we register particularly clearly through regular sacramental confession is that the life of faith is not so much a matter of observable self-improvement as a prolonged education in humility, a matter of having to confess the same uninteresting and devastatingly ordinary sins again and again, and learning to accept and live with this self that does not seem to advance very much.[2] It is a characteristic element in the Christian realism. The classical list of the seven deadly sins is as accurate and shrewd a summary of essential human weakness for our day as it was for a thousand years ago. It was this feature of sin, its monotonous and boring quality, that produced from the sensitive mind of Baudelaire the irreplaceable image 'Le spectacle ennuyeux de l'immortel péché'.[3] Beauty and goodness have an eternal freshness, they spring up in new forms and original grace in every generation. The appalling thing about sin is that man does not appear to be able to create in that realm, it is always the same old thing man has been doing all along. The idea of observable self-improvement does not seem to be part of the Christian way—it goes with the *Reader's Digest* but

[1] A valuable analysis of Christian teaching about confession illustrated by a study of T. S. Eliot's *Ash Wednesday* is found in *Mastery and Mercy* by P. M. Martin, pp. 75–145.

[2] Reginald Cant, *The Churchman's Companion*, p. 214. Canon Cant's chapter in this otherwise indifferent book is a model of pastoral counsel.

[3] Charles Baudelaire, *Les Fleurs du Mal; Le Voyage.*

not the New Testament. I believe myself to be speaking from within Christian faith when I say that one just gets to know oneself and finds that one can live with this self-knowledge in the realm of grace, that is to say, knowing that one is accepted by God and that his presence makes each returning day a thing of hope and joy. This is what Jesus meant by 'going down to one's house justified'.

It is part of the Christian idea that this is possible, that it is possible to go forward into life with a creative view of what has happened and an infinitely hopeful outlook on the future. In Christ the two infinities of past and future meet in a now that is good. When sin is forgiven it becomes the bearer of a kind of light. 'The moment the prodigal son fell on his knees and wept he made his past sacred moments in his life.'[1] 'The true meaning of confession is that it is the consequence of the renewal which Jesus Christ brings; its secret is that Christ is Lord even of the wasted years of the past.'[2] And as for the future, through forgiveness it is possible to reach the point of being

> Able to approach the Future as a friend
> Without a wardrobe of excuses, without
> A set mask of rectitude or an
> Embarrassing over-familiar gesture.

And this openness to the future is encouraged by another element in forgiveness which Auden indicates in the same poem, the fact that we now see more clearly

> . . . what evil is: not, as we thought,
> Deeds that must be punished, but our lack of faith,
> Our dishonest mood of denial. . . .[3]

But it is just about as difficult to do this on one's own as it is for a neurotic to make that journey into the interior which becomes a possibility for him only with the help of a competent analyst.

The fact is that, in the Christian view, we were never meant to attempt it on our own, but in the community of faith. John Wesley wrote to one of his preachers: 'If you press all the believers

---

[1] E. Lampert, *The Apocalypse of History*, p. 66.
[2] Von Allmen, *Vocabulary of the Bible*, p. 64.
[3] W. H. Auden, 'In Memory of Sigmund Freud' (Penguin Poets), p. 69.

to go on to perfection and to expect deliverance from sin every moment, they will grow in grace. But if ever they lose that expectation they will grow flat and cold.' But this perfection, holiness, plenitude of loving (all synonymous in Methodist spirituality) is not merely something beyond us. It is in part something we live in now, in the Church, in that we belong to that holy company of faith which God called into being in Christ. The holiness that is already ours by membership in the Body is appropriated and developed personally as the mind is renewed by Christian truth and sacramental grace. But none of this can happen without such relationship of intimacy, candour and confidence as obtains between confessor and penitent, in the dialogue of pastoral counselling, in the friendship in Christ of class leader and member. The religious life of people in the twentieth century is going to be helped as much, if not more, by various forms of this personal intimacy along with the sacramental life, as it was a century ago by the great preaching services and the vigorous general fellowship of the Church. Today the mass meeting is finished; even the sermon in the Sunday worship of the Church is on the whole a pathetic failure. Some form of conversation with a spiritual director (though 'director' is a ghastly word), at any rate the kind of spiritual relationship which is based on conversation and intimate personal communication, is the way believers of our day are going to learn Christ.

To many Methodists this opinion may be uncongenial. But they should remember that John Wesley at first encouraged the practice of a kind of confessional in the early class meetings.[1] This has been a feature of Christian earnestness and honesty in the many small groups seeking holiness that have repeatedly come into existence in Christian history from earliest times down to the first form of the Oxford Group (now abysmally degenerated into M.R.A.). But in every instance the practice has died, and for obvious reasons. It needs, for maximum effectiveness and minimum danger, to be safeguarded by ecclesiastical structure; it needs a tradition of spiritual direction, a certain privacy on the human level, and the authority and wisdom of the Church to sift sin from scruple, to say what is and is not penitence, and to give

---

[1] Cf. F. Greeves, introducing *Confession* by Max Thurian (publ. S.C.M.). This book is particularly useful for Christians unfamiliar with the tradition of sacramental confession.

the penitent the assurance that he is forgiven and can go in peace. And this we cannot provide from ourselves for ourselves.

It will always be true that any penitent confessing in solitary prayer can be assured of forgiveness. It is also true that this stupendous bit of Christian orthodoxy often does not work out into anything anyone could honour with the word peace and particularly when that peace is most needed. Perhaps it is due to the fact that there is something inescapably social about Christianity; everything happens within this banished privacy called the Body of Christ. It is not good for man to be alone, especially with his sins. And those traditions that have retained the sacrament of penance would seem to be nearer the truth and comfort of Christ than those that have let this means of grace go. Of course, it is all extremely personal, and some people prefer a less personal kind of faith; but some will want it personal to the uttermost limits of the self—*my* sins absolved, *my present condition* spoken to by a minister offering God's counsel to *me* and no one else, to me who have just told him how it is with me.

Certainly many Methodist ministers seem to be increasingly hungry nowadays at least for the spiritual direction of which this sacrament is in part a means. The minister is usually the most unhelped man in the circuit. There are some who want this sacrament in its fullest significance and blessing and seek it elsewhere. A further benefit is the essential education in pastoral sympathy that a minister derives from bringing his spiritual need to a priest and hearing this brother in Christ say just what in his spiritual condition is given him to say as counsel. It is not always interesting, it is not always helpful, though sometimes it miraculously speaks to one's condition. And this situation is exactly that which obtains between flock and pastor. They want so much, but he can only give them what God can give him in his present condition of fidelity or infidelity, and at times this is little enough. It is necessary to the ministry of the minister that he realize this to the full; and it can only be realized by being actually in the situation of spiritual need and receiving just what God can at that moment give through some ordained but ignorant and sinful servant in the ordered life of the Church and having faith that in some sense this is God's word, to be listened to with attention, to be looked all over expectantly for that bit of relevance that could be grace. When the minister has this discipline in his regular life he will better understand what the layman has to do if he is going to get anywhere with the faith, and what, in his minister, he has to bear with and even at times forgive.

5

Desiring Good for Oneself

THE prayer that asks God to act, to fill some gap in our happiness or make good something we consider bad, is the most difficult prayer to use. Unless it rises from the deepest level of religious life, where God is praised and thanked and life is understood as the offering of the self to him in communion and service, it is in the Christian view very likely to be the wrong use of praying.

Not that it is wrong to want happiness. Nothing more worth wanting and seeking can be imagined. Christianity is about happiness, our painful thirst for it, and what chances there are of finding it. Indeed this has always been the steady theme in the religious mind of man.

It seems that the removal of self-concern is an extremely important issue because self-concern inhibits love. When one's attention is directed to achieving narrowly personal goals, or life is experienced as in the main a series of threats from which the self must be protected so that one can objectively appreciate the world only when one feels safe, the chances of happiness are minimal. The mind's freedom is restricted in a narrow and exhausting pattern of defensiveness and aggressiveness in which its power to love cannot function.

Consequently it is reasonable to suppose that happiness consists, at any rate in considerable part, in reducing our defensiveness and aggressiveness to that point at which they are no longer compulsive but simply constitute energy to be drawn on whenever there is something rightly to be defended or attacked. This relaxes the mind and gives our loving room and freedom to function. The more and the more profoundly people love the happier they are, as Christianity understands happiness.

But these ideas are not originally Christian nor now uniquely so. They are assumed and taught, with greater or less emphasis, in the writings of all the major religions.[1] They are given enduring expression in much of the world's poetry; and their domain extends further still, into the consulting rooms of doctors and psychiatrists, whose patients are there more because of the causal connection between blocked loving and illness than for any other single reason; so that they begin to have the familiar look associated with the facts of life.

Religion is the attempt to live life according to the facts, according to how things are. The purpose of prayer is to train the mind to function in accordance with the facts and, incidentally but most importantly, in accordance with the facts about happiness, that is to say, affectionately and freely, not defensively and aggressively, but turned appreciatively outward towards that which is not the self. And the not-self is of course God and the world of persons and things.

Accordingly private prayer is principally a matter of thinking and reading about the Christian image of the free and happy life (Jesus Christ), understanding its implications, intensifying one's desire for it, seeing one's experience in terms of it, and all this in order to free the mind and direct it for loving as many persons and things as possible and responding creatively to events, because this is the way one loves God, the only way God can be loved in this world.

That is the purpose of prayer, to help one to love. The praying itself is 'exercise towards' loving, 'reflection in depth' on what God and life and love are as understood in the Christian tradition. It is part of this teaching that life reaches its fulfilment of meaning and joy as God rules in men's responding hearts and they do his will. God's purpose is to bring about this fulfilment of life. Indeed this is what is happening all the time. Life *is* God fulfilling his purpose and doing so in love and by love.

All that the Christian can do therefore, all he can conceivably *want* to do, is to thank God that this is so and ask to be taken into it and share it. To ask for the good things of God's kingdom is to offer oneself to God's rule. So that Christian prayer is the opposite of magic. Magic uses prayers and liturgical forms of one kind and another to persuade or influence God to act in a certain way to meet the wishes of the suppliant. The Christian in prayer does not wish to persuade God to do anything other than what he is in fact

[1] Cf. Aldous Huxley, *The Perennial Philosophy*, ch. 6.

continually doing—fulfilling his purpose in love. He simply wants himself to participate more fully in what God is doing. His prayer both expresses this want and furthers its realization.

If the Christian wants 'things' altered, the appropriate course would not seem to be prayer but some action to modify the situation he wants altered. If he cannot do anything to change the undesired circumstances, he then has to endure this frustration and disappointment and find a way of viewing them that is productive of life and not destructive. That is certainly a situation in which prayer is extremely relevant. But prayer is not for 'getting things done' in the usual sense of those words. It is no help at all to think of God as 'a source of causative action in the world of phenomena to be reckoned as additional and external to those agencies which he has brought into being in the wills of men' so that our prayer is 'an attempt to make up for our own deficiency in power or wisdom by calling that other more reliable Agent into operation for the accomplishment of what seems to us good'.[1]

It is likely that the more Christian one's praying is the more regular it will be. The more spasmodic and intermittent it is and the more it tends to be something one resorts to only in crisis, the more likely it will be that it is nearer to magical formula than Christian prayer. 'The more tenuous the relation between the prayer and the rest of the person's life, the more suspect the prayer becomes.'[1]

It is often suggested that if we cannot tell God anything he does not know and if we have abandoned the thought of him as a power to be engaged in the interests of some good our mind proposes, there seems little point in praying at all.

But if you take out of praying the operations of informing and using God you do not empty it. You merely remove from it the veil of misunderstanding and self-regarding manipulation that have concealed its true use from you.

It does seem, however, that what remains when this conventional veil is removed is some elemental form of asking for the accomplishment of God's will and allying oneself with it. And it is true that the great exponents of prayer in all mature religions do tend towards such extreme simplicity in their regular prayer.

[1] John Burnaby, *Soundings* (ed. Vidler), p. 232.
[2] D. Z. Phillips, *The Concept of Prayer*, p. 115.

Indeed, the deepest prayer always moves through the steady reduction of the need of words to the condition of silence. But it is the opposite of an empty silence. It is not 'a mere cessation of speech, it is something positive like love, death and life. It is not a pause between noises, sermons and theological disquisitions, but something without which words lose their meaning and turn into sounds made with the mere intention of being audible'.[1]

But this is not the state of prayer and love of God which most of us have reached, though in some moment of beautiful or dreadful truth we may indeed see that there is nothing to *say*. But in the ordinary run of experience the great weakness in simplifying our prayers before we have developed a profound understanding of what is meant by 'the accomplishment of God's purpose' is that we shall probably find ourselves praying for nothing in particular and soon not praying at all. We are beings whose lives are continually pulled this way and that by the complicated currents of particular desires. We want this, then, as we surrender our individuality to process, we want that, then something else—some of it good, some of it very far from good to us or anyone, some of it we in any case cannot have except insubstantially in the disappointing fantasy-world to which the mind compensatingly runs when life is unsupportable. If we pray about all these things, including even those foolish things we know we want only with the superficial and maybe discreditable part of ourselves—and by 'praying about' is meant 'bring into our thought about God'—we sanctify ourselves as persons who desire this (and wish we did not) and then that (and wish we could so desire more often). And this means that we bring that life of desire into the light of God's truth, where it is criticized and purified and set in orderly relation to the deepest desire we can possibly have, the desire that flows like a secret river underneath all our life—that God's will may be done and that we may belong to his reality.[2]

But as time goes on, though we may never reach the condition of simplicity of a St. Teresa (who found eventually that the two words 'Our Father' contained all that the praying mind needs to centre round) or of that tradition in Orthodoxy that finds one brief sentence, the 'Jesus prayer', sufficient, there will certainly

[1] Eugeny Lampert, *The Orthodox Ethos*, vol. 1, p. 222.
[2] Cf. Dom Christopher Butler, *Prayer, an adventure in living*, pp. 21–2.

be a reduction of the variety and multiplicity of want in our minds when we seek to address God. For example, it is incredible that twentieth-century Christians in the western world should still wish to pray for good weather and that this wish should be provided for in recent liturgical revisions.[1]

The Christian convert who wants to know what are the words one can legitimately say to God can be told that this is one need for which Christ certainly provided. One of the characteristic instructions about prayer that Jesus gave his disciples was that they were to pray 'in his name'. Because in the Bible the 'name' means 'the person' this means that Christian prayer is part of our being 'in Christ'. It is the sort of thing we say to God and want to say to God when we share, as much as we are able, Jesus's commitment to the Father, his concern for God's rule in the world, his faith in God's providential care, and the rest of the Jesus view of life and its meaning. Whenever we even begin to get into this condition of enlightenment and self-offering, half the prayers we thought of praying die on our lips; they become either irrelevant or impossible. You begin to wonder whether you can say anything that makes sense other than that you wish to be truly surrendered to God and that you deplore everything in you that keeps you from him.

Actually there is not much that one can say. But what one can say is of great importance in defining what the Christian religion is about. And Jesus left us in no doubt about this. It is all in the Lord's Prayer. What is written there is what Christians believe can and should be said to God. This is why the exposition of the Lord's Prayer is extremely important in the life of the Church from generation to generation. Every Christian should attend to any help that is going towards understanding it.[2]

It is no part of the purpose of this book to expound this prayer. But it is important to note here that in the attitude to life that Jesus adopted it seems there is no point in objecting to God, to calling in question what he does and allows, though in extremity we cannot stop ourselves doing this. You can only say 'Hallowed be thy name', that is to say, may all men regard God's name, his

[1] *Alternative Services*, 2nd Series, S.P.C.K., p. 63.

[2] E.g. Joachim Jeremias, *The Prayers of Jesus*; Evelyn Underhill, *Abba*; Gerhard Ebeling, *The Lord's Prayer in Today's World*; Simone Weil, *Concerning the Our Father* (in *Waiting on God*); Raissa Maritain, *Notes sur le Pater*; Archbishop Anthony Bloom, *Living Prayer*; Ernst Lohmeyer, *The Lord's Prayer*.

being, the way things are, as holy, as providential and right and the revelation of an infinite love; or, if they cannot reach this fantastic viewpoint now, may they be led by the divine Spirit to that point of experience when they can. It is certainly an extraordinary point of view. It means that all the unaccountable time before man appeared on the earth, when all the names of history were unknown, and the being who spoke of God with the familiarity and *naïveté* of the word 'Abba', who revealed himself to God in the words of St. Augustine's *Confessions*, who created King Lear and composed Beethoven's last quartets, was something crawling out of some ghostly sea and trying to get a foothold on to something that did not move with the tides, down through all the blood and beauty of history until now, all that time and process are to be thought of as Love fulfilling one purpose, the deepest possible happiness of man.

After this there is nothing else to say but 'Thy kingdom come, thy will be done'; may men increasingly acknowledge and accept God's rule in their lives and the world, and do what he wants them to do, because what he wants them to do is one form or another of love. And whatever they do, may I have the sense, the understanding, the grace to do this, to see life in this way, because, though it certainly does not look like it, this is the truth about it.

The rest of the pattern prayer completes the basic form that Christian asking may rightly take. The words 'on earth as it is in heaven' imply that the Christian must hold in the mind both the conviction that God is in fact fulfilling his purpose and the sensitive awareness that that purpose is not yet fulfilled in time, and all the pain and question this awareness excites. The daily bread, the forgiveness, the guidance, the deliverance from evil complete the exemplary concepts in which Jesus taught that God is rightly addressed and can be expectantly trusted to respond to anyone so approaching him.

If this seems too austere, as no doubt it will to many people, they have only to ask themselves what else they can possibly want from God as they stand before him in Christ. Of course we want many other things than this mysterious bread and the guidance and the forgiveness, and some of them are admirable wants. But the question is do we want to make a point of asking God for them in Christ? If we do, then we must unashamedly and unselfconsciously pray in that way. 'Pray as you can, and do not try to pray as you can't. Take yourself as you find yourself, and start from that.'[1]

But to pray in the name of Christ means to share his way of looking at life. And this must gradually change the desires we want to lift up to God, and ultimately our whole life of desire. We cannot continue our 'learning Christ' within the worship and teaching of the Church and not expect inner change to begin. The place where that change first makes itself felt is our life of wanting. We begin to feel the importance drain away from some wants, which are in fact dying. Some wants still burn within us, and we know that God knows their power over us, but our release from them is in fact heralded by the realization that they look incongruous alongside the ideas about life and its meaning that Jesus's mind continually ruminated, and we do not want now to bring them into our prayers unless it be to ask for release from them. In time we notice our prayers of asking for ourselves growing shorter and simpler. And it is not long before we find ourselves thinking that all we truly want to ask for ourselves from God is God and the grace to do his will. There is certainly nothing else worth asking for. He has nothing else to give.

The fact remains that we do find ourselves in certain situations asking for things God cannot give. There is a long tradition of association between prayer and crisis; for example, when someone is very ill and the doctors seem beaten, or in moments of danger when our own or someone else's life is threatened, or on other occasions of personal or national calamity or decision. Such experiences call up from the depths of the mind the little frightened child everyone carries within, and when man becomes an infant crying in the night he has no language but a cry. There is no point in adopting a superior attitude to the self as under strain it regresses to a level on which we hoped the mind would not again find itself grovelling. This happens, and it must be accepted with charity towards oneself. But we are functioning then as frightened humans not as trusting Christians. As Christians we know that we must be ready for all his perfect will; that is to say, we know that the worst could happen and that what matters is not what happens but our doing God's will in it. Accordingly, spiritual growth invariably implies movement away from fear of life towards a condition of trusting God and wanting to serve him

[1] Dom John Chapman, *Spiritual Letters*, p. 109.

whichever way the cards fall. 'The prayer of petition is best understood, not as an attempt at influencing the way things go, but as an expression of, and a request for, devotion to God through the way things go.'[1]

The purification of desire, the education of human wanting, is one of the principal ways in which God answers prayer. It is always a reduction, which reaches its culmination in the single desire for God himself and his kingdom.

It seems that Jesus's criticism of 'vain repetitions' was not a criticism of the use of repetition in prayer. Repetition has always had and will always have an extremely important place in the life of prayer. Indeed, the more the asceticism of asking progresses in the Christian life, the more we shall want to repeat the few phrases we finally consider worth uttering in God's presence. Jesus's criticism of vain repetitions appears to have been connected closely with pagan practice: 'use not vain repetitions *as the Gentiles do*, for they think they shall be heard for their much speaking'.[2] In pagan prayer there used to be long and involved invocations, calling all conceivable gods in order that you might persuade at least one to listen; and it was also a matter of anxiety that you should address the god with his right title. The sentence may be interpreted as criticizing the idea of a lot of talk intended to impress God by its very volume. So the words are translated in the Revised Standard Version 'do not heap up empty phrases', in Ronald Knox's version 'do not use many phrases', in the New English Bible 'do not go babbling on'.[3] What is being criticized is obviously not the principle of repetition in prayer, much less the regular use of a written liturgy, but elaborate verbosity. Indeed the criticism is much more relevant to much old-style non-conformist extempore prayer in which the conventional phrases go on and on and, as the years pass, seem increasingly empty of meaning. It is certainly the case that we have so little evidence of the prayer life of Jesus that it is impossible to say in any detail how he prayed. But the evidence we have is all marvellously brief, simple and succinct; and this characteristic is preserved much more successfully in the best collects in the *Book of Common Prayer*

---

[1] D. Z. Phillips, *The Concept of Prayer*, pp. 120–1.

[2] Matt. vi, 7. (R.Y.)

[3] St. John Chrysostom interpreted the phrase in this way and explained 'babbling' as 'asking from God what is not properly to be asked from him'. Cf. Panagiotis C. Trembelas, *The Orthodox Ethos*, pp. 122 ff.

than in the 'free' prayer of those Christian traditions that have somehow sensed a mysterious and holy 'mystique' in the unscripted prayer.

It is true that the extempore prayer of some devout examples of the free tradition in the old days was wonderful to hear. The author remembers vividly from his youth his father's prayers at family prayer—saturated in the imagery of the Authorized Version, the phrases or thoughts of Shakespeare, Pascal and Newman, and the original ideas of a man who naturally thought aloud about God in the sense that the thought found vocal form immediately, but this kind of expertise is rarely found today in the Free Church tradition.

But this verbal 'ascesis' is much less important than the actual reduction of what one wants from God and life. Each generation has to work out for itself a form of holiness relevant to and viable in its time. This involves re-thinking the theology of petition, making some attempt at saying what, under God, a Christian may reasonably desire in his generation and how much of his generation's desiring and needing he ought, in Christ, to suspect. Not enough is done to help Christians in this matter. Such attempts as are made are either too erudite and academic or else so obviously the product of contemporary pietism that only those on that particular 'spiritual wavelength' can derive any help from it. It is part of the contemporary '*trahison des clercs*' that so much of the help that is offered to Christian people comes either from the erudite or the pietist. Many Christians cannot take the Church's counsel in either of these forms—one is incomprehensible, the other is nauseating—and the result is that while the official flock decreases the hungry sheep that look up and are not fed increase rapidly.

However, there have been some attempts to make clear the shape a mid-twentieth-century holiness might take. One of the more serviceable is provided by a short essay by Canon V. A. Demant.[1] He suggests that a framework for a twentieth-century holiness might consist of (*a*) the readiness to bear the trials of existence as part of our acceptance of our creatureliness, (*b*) respect for the 'givenness of things', i.e. material things, and the bases of life in families, traditions, institutions, cultures, histories, (*c*) 'some conscious discrimination between the multifarious

[1] In *Christian Spirituality Today* (Ed. the Archbishop of Canterbury), pp. 50–5.

stimuli offered to our minds and hearts, and the refusal to be subject to a good many of them', (*d*) finding ways of securing occasions for solitude and thought, (*e*) acquiring resistance to 'the insidious commercial propaganda to increase our wants' (we need a religious 'discipline as consumers'), (*f*) an accepted form of renunciation which would encourage young people 'to seek occupations which, though not so financially rewarding as others, are worth while because they meet the uncorrupted requirements of their fellowmen', and (*g*) an understanding, in a world of affluence and full employment, of the right use of unemployed time.

Some recent attempts at saying what holiness might be for our time consider the way in which the traditional Christian triad of self-offering (poverty, chastity and obedience) may find convincing expression in twentieth-century life. It is suggested that this will work out in the assertion that life is more than *the possession of things* and that the ability to do without the much-advertised things of this world is part of the freedom of Christ. It will involve the conviction that satisfied sexuality is a matter of two human beings walking hand in hand into that realm where, for both, the ego with its demands is offered in sacrifice to love. And it will involve the idea of an obedience from which some people will refuse to be diverted. 'The health of any society depends on there being those in it who will say in the last resort: "We must obey God rather than man", and are prepared in principle to sacrifice life itself for their impertinence.'[1]

Another version of holiness that has power in our time derives from the work of Charles de Foucauld. He was primarily concerned with a desert tribe in North Africa, the most abandoned people he could find. His followers have accordingly chosen to work among the cares, worries and uncertainties of those who do not know Christ. Many European cities come into this category as well as the Sahara. And the Little Brothers and Sisters who derive their inspiration from him frequently work in the vast loneliness and impersonality of the great cities of Europe and they strive to avoid everything that cuts them off from those among whom they live and work.[2]

There are other movements in Christendom today which seek

[1] G. E. Hudson, *The Arts of Sacrifice*, in *The Listener*, 1st September 1960.
[2] Cf. R. Voillaume, *Seeds of the Desert*, a study of the legacy of Charles de Foucauld.

this identification with ordinary people, this sharing of their temptations, joys and griefs. It seems that it is along these lines that a twentieth-century lay holiness is to be worked out. Certainly those forms of devout life in the Church which are simply the attempt to keep a few church members together or to interest them so that they mutually adhere, the cultivation of Christian fellowship for its own sake, to assuage the loneliness of people who ought not to be lonely if they have learned anything of Christ, all this we now realize is to be thrown on the religious scrap-heap. It has nothing to do with holiness. It is Christian self-indulgence. The only fellowship that is the fellowship of the Spirit is that in which Christians are gathered together in worship (once a week, on Sunday, is enough), in study of the Bible or Christian faith, or in service to the community. Life is much too short, and too serious, for the cultivation of Christian fellowship for the sake of Christian fellowship. Indeed much of local church 'togetherness' is a waste of time.

6

Resenting

THE more deeply we understand what Christians are doing when in Christ they ask for some good for themselves, the more we find ourselves calling in question the entire world of our ordinary wanting. That complex world is the familiar clamour of conflicting wants in whose distraction we struggle to live. When we look within we can find ourselves wanting what is good, beautiful, amusing and life-enhancing, and also and just as powerfully what will certainly not satisfy us, may even destroy us, what is quite inconsistent with the way we most deeply desire to live our lives, and also what in any case we can never have.

This tantalizing realm of desiring is fed in part by two great streams of mental life, our resentments and our fears. It cannot be simplified until something is done about these.

Anyone who begins the Christian life soon observes, with surprise and dismay, the hindrance constituted by all the inner stream of dislike, complaint, criticism, anger, envy, cynicism which flows through our silent thoughts when we are doing nothing in particular, and sometimes when we are involved in activity as well. Christian holiness (the principal 'remote preparation' for prayer) must clearly have something to do with getting rid of all this useless living and replacing it with love. God cannot answer any prayer until this negative emotion begins to disperse and some room is made in the mind for God and the joy of life. One of the points in the unfortunately brief instruction on prayer which Jesus gave is that a forgiving mind is an essential condition to being answered by God. Life itself, as well as people, must be forgiven. You need not have a single personal enemy you can name but you can hate life bitterly all the same.

The elimination of resentment involves some conscious attention to the whole problem of our aggressiveness whose deep and diverse roots we certainly have not the insight to trace out. But of the many discernible connections within the self there is an important one linking resentment with inertia.

It is obvious that all of us have a deep resistance to life—to life as a living, moving thing that takes us unawares, drags us out of the familiar into situations in which we have got to think or go under. Once our life is reasonably well organized we want it to stay like that, we want to be left in peace. We are disturbed, if things begin to move, simply because they move. And when things go wrong it is probable that a good deal of our agitation has been set in motion in the first place simply because the *status quo* has been disturbed by the appearance of unexpected difficulties. We are secretly angry that the cards have not continued to fall as we think they ought to fall. This kind of resentment can be lessened, certainly will be lessened, as we learn something about what Christians call 'poverty of spirit', the essential letting-go which comes first in the catalogue of the beatitudes. If we crucify the clutching self and learn to sit loose to life, accepting its uncertain onset as it comes instead of expecting it to arrange itself neatly and according to our wishes, the flow of the mind's incessant conversation with itself will certainly be more peaceful. We shall have the further advantage, when reverses come, of being emotionally free to focus our attention on what really matters, that is to say, on what God wants us to *do* in them and with them.

Another important relation is that between resentment and self-esteem. Christians believe that human beings were made for love, for oneness with life. To approach things and people with interest and affection generally means spiritual growth. To approach them with hostility, to stand away from life and look it up and down and hit at it with some verbal weapon means decay. The personality shrivels up. The more our personalities are withdrawn and moribund, the more insignificant we feel. Then usually follow more criticism, more hostility to life, more resentment, partly because we are angry that life is so uncongenial, but also because such aggression gives the impoverished self a temporary sense of power and meaning. Much uncharitableness is the humiliated ego's attempt to feed its self-esteem by hostility.

This root of resentment can be cut only by humility, by the conviction that meaning is something that is *given* to life by God. Humility is so deep a word that it is almost another word for religion in the Christian view. It means that 'we are heartily content that He appoint us our place and work, and that He alone be our reward'.[1] Simone Weil saw this so clearly that she was able to say 'humility is the refusal to exist outside God'.

Resentment may be directed against people (including oneself) or against God. Resentment against people can be traced to three principal sources.

The first is undissolved anger. When we are hurt by someone our first natural reaction is anger and the desire for revenge. A number of factors generally prevent this immediate expression of hostility. The person who has injured us may be someone we love, or we may not see any adequate means of retaliation, or our moral ideal may not allow revenge. This situation, in which anger and some restraining force are in evenly-balanced opposition within us, is emotionally painful. And it is often this that most hurts when we say on such occasions 'I feel terribly hurt'. It is necessary that something be done about it as soon as possible. If nothing is done, the situation simply recedes into our memory as an undigested painful experience and remains there, a hard lump of conflict that will not disperse. And whenever we see the person concerned, or indeed anything that reminds us of the original situation, we shall feel the pain of it over and over again. The painful experience must be dealt with as soon as possible. If we cannot, or will not let ourselves, express our anger, we must dissolve it. Various reflections help to dissolve anger, making allowances for the person who has injured us, realizing that no act deserves continual ill-will, reminding ourselves of our own endless need of forgiveness, reaffirming our belief that the Christian religion is as much about forgiveness as about anything else. It is also useful to recognize how exhausting hostility is.

The second source of resentment is pride. All of us carry around a certain number of illusions and irrational claims. It is inevitable that we shall feel resentment when these are challenged. Accordingly, we should look at our resentments with some care, to see how many are justifiable and how many are really due to the vulnerability that we have built up by our many irrational claims and sensitivenesses. We shall always feel hurt if others do something that hurts our pride or fail to do

[1] The Methodist Covenant Service, *The Book of Offices*, p. 131.

something that our pride requires. It is unlikely that we shall make any progress in loving without the systematic reduction of all this unnecessary vulnerability. One of the commonest illusions of human pride is the conviction that to withhold forgiveness, to persist in resentment, is a form of asserting strength and even of effective retaliation. Actually this strategy not only maintains the pain of the injury, by keeping it in the centre of awareness, it also intensifies it, by adding to it the strain of mental conflict because we are secretly conscious of the futility, if not also the wrongness, of what we are doing. This kind of pain can only be dispelled by forgiveness. But to be able to forgive one must renounce many of the claims and illusions to which one is clinging. We cling to them for the allaying of anxiety and the production of security, but quite hopelessly because they merely increase vulnerability. It is not sufficiently understood by Christian believers how important the tragic world of pride is in the Christian theory of evil.

The other principal source of resentment is the disappointment of extravagant expectations. Dostoevsky and Coleridge both came to the conclusion that, in Shakespeare's play, Othello did not kill Desdemona because he was jealous but because he was robbed of his ideal. The conviction that she had fallen from the pedestal of exalted innocence and perfection on which he had always mysteriously needed to set her flung him into an unbearable rage, against her and against life. In the small dramas of everyday human unhappiness extravagant expectations generally play a role whose importance is all the greater for being rarely recognized.

In the life of holiness the sentimental mind has never had the criticism it deserves. There is a common lack of imagination and realism about human beings which must be considered part of the whole world of pretence that is foreign to love. If love, as St. Paul said, rejoices in the truth, we should understand that other people (including those we most deeply love, into whose personalities we are inclined to overestimate our insight) are just as easily provoked and frightened as we are. All people tend to react foolishly, even cruelly, when they are provoked or frightened. There is nothing people will not do under sufficient pressure and strain. It is not love but the failure of love to exempt certain people in any way from the possibility of evil. To love one's neighbour as oneself means to love him as a person like oneself, a human being whose possibilities for good and for evil are immense. The love that dare not look at life's dark potentiality is not love at all, it is fear.

But no person has ever been hated as much as God. There are many people who have no special quarrel with particular individuals but burn with a chronic resentment against the general treatment they have received at the hands of life. This is rage against God.

In the Christian tradition it is believed that the whole course of things in this world is within the fatherly providence of God. Sometimes this fatherliness is obvious to faith, sometimes it is completely hidden; but, whatever its appearance, all life is *always* within that fatherliness. When we are angry at what happens to us we are angry with God.

This means that we think we have claims on God, that, for example, he should arrange life to meet our wishes, or maintain our enjoyments, or reward our efforts, or compensate us for our pains. This attitude is completely foreign to the mind of Jesus.[1]

When we begin to pray in Christ's name we begin to realize the many un-Christian assumptions and claims that have become part of our automatic response to life. We know we are involved in a long task of getting rid of them and learning to accept. It is hard to think of any part of the Christian concept of holiness that is more rewarding or more relevant to our time. There are so many disappointed and querulous people in the western world, with all its means of joy, that it is difficult to exaggerate the harvest of liberation and happiness waiting to be gathered by anyone prepared to practise Christian teaching on abandonment to providence.[2]

But the inflexible and demanding ego has been resisting the dismaying side of life so long that practice is necessary if it is ever going to learn how to trust and obey. Such practice, at any rate as the saints have sketched it out, has always included regular exercises in the acceptance of disappointments and difficulties, and the seeking of God's will in them. At the centre of

---

[1] R. Bultmann, *Jesus and the Word* (Fontana Books), pp. 122–3.
[2] Cf. *Abandonment to Divine Providence*, J. P. de Caussade (The Catholic Records Press, Exeter). This book is essential reading for all who wish to understand Christian praying.

the Christian life is the Cross, a completely new valuation of pain and what is to be done with it.

> Expect contradiction and opposition, together with crosses of various kinds. Consider the words of St Paul: 'To you it is given in the behalf of Christ'—for his sake, as a fruit of his death and intercession for you—'not only to believe, but also to suffer for his sake' (Phil. i, 29). 'It is given'. God gives you this opposition or reproach; it is a fresh token of his love. And will you disown the giver or spurn his gift, and count it a misfortune? Will you not rather say, 'Father the hour is come that thou shouldest be glorified; now thou givest thy child to suffer something for thee; do with me according to thy will'? Know that these things, far from being hindrances to the work of God, or to your soul, are not only unavoidable in the course of providence, but profitable, yea necessary, for you. Therefore, receive them from God (not from chance) with willingness, with thankfulness.

The passage is from Wesley's *Plain Account of Christian Perfection*. It could come, almost without alteration, from the writings of St. Francis de Sales or St. Teresa or Fénélon, or indeed any of the principal voices in the tradition of Christian spirituality.

The more Christian believers find their faith dealing with the problem of their resentments the more they will escape the peculiar torpor of the twentieth century. Resentment ultimately degenerates into listlessness. Genuine revolt against genuine evil, because it is not merely negative but the outcome of a positive adherence to some good which gives it energy, can fight and work without tiring. Mere resentment ultimately sinks into a sullen inertia. There is much of this inertia in the society of our time. It is indeed the contemporary version of the sin of sloth, and it has many causes, some of which we are not yet able to identify.

Part of the cause is the standardization of life that inevitably accompanies a successful mass-production economy. The sameness of existence and the silence about ideals produce a universal boredom made up of social indifference, torpid conformity, a general *taedium vitae*. There are of course many attempts to escape from this huge dullness, from the awakened interest in Victoriana to destruction for its own sake or the craze for experimentation in sensation, dream or hallucination under the influence of drugs. From the world of the theatre and the novel appears evidence that as a generation we may be unable to make attempts at solving the riddle of life and prefer to frighten ourselves with horrifying assertions of life's meaninglessness.

There is of course a general sense of impotence in the twentieth-century mind, of being at the mercy of unidentifiable forces in international affairs, community life, and in oneself. In any case, people between the ages of 25 and 50 tend normally to be beset with misgivings, questions, loss of enthusiasm as the tide of youth ebbs out. Actually, this is no tragedy, because in normal spiritual growth the tide returns, if one is ready to receive it, bringing new and more mature thoughts of life which revitalize a self content to be a creature of time as well as of eternity. But the great decline of religious confidence in our day makes this renewal a less likely development for more people.

These circumstances issue in an impoverishment of the self that amounts to a deep personal uncertainty. Much in the art of this century suggests that this condition is increasing. The plays of Samuel Beckett, the paintings of Francis Bacon, the novels of Kafka and his many imitators, all seem to concern people who are uncertain about who they are, who live without feeling alive, who feel they can only continue on a basis of pretence, pretending there is a meaning to existence but unable to take even the pretence seriously—like Mr. Harold Pinter's caretaker who is always saying that he must go down to Sidcup to get his papers (the papers which establish his *bona fide* identity) but never gets round to making the journey. This pretence and uncertainty form a pervasive fog in which much of life is being lived just now. We may even fabricate it ourselves to relieve us of the responsibility of seeing clearly.

7

Fearing

WE shall not make much advance in simplifying and reducing our desires, so that the desire for God and his kingdom has a chance with us, unless we attempt to understand some of the things we fear.

Fears give some indication of what, sometimes quite unconsciously, we consider necessary for our existence, because they register areas of wanting that are being threatened.

As we learn to live by faith we are less afraid of life and therefore we have less wants whose purpose is the allaying of anxiety.

Holiness is in part the right use of power. There is a right way and a wrong way of using our power of thought and imagination. When we are faced with a problem, if our thinking about it is constructive and leads to some decision to act, we are presumably using the power of thought in the right way. When the decision has been made, all that then remains for us to do is to put the decision into action. Should we discover that no action is possible or necessary for the present, any further brooding on the matter is a misuse of the mind, and we should turn our minds to other topics. If the worry returns, we should disengage our minds from it with the reflection that we have done all the fruitful thinking we can about that particular matter for the time being.

'Sufficient not only unto the day, but also unto the place, is the evil thereof. Agitation over happenings which we are powerless to modify, either because they have not yet occurred, or else are occurring at an inaccessible distance from us, achieves nothing beyond the inoculation of here and now with the remote or anticipated evil that is the object of our distress.'[1]

It also paralyses the will, so that we are prevented from doing what God wants us to do in this particular hour because we are

[1] Aldous Huxley, *The Perennial Philosophy* (Fontana Books), p. 113.

too preoccupied to think about anything as objective as God's will, or too depressed to be interested in it.

The will of God is always something we are to do *now*, in this present moment, because the present moment is the only moment in which we can do anything. Accordingly, any voluntary behaviour which prevents us from seeing and doing God's will in the present situation, in the Christian view, comes into the category of sin.[1]

> The care that is filling your mind at this moment or but waiting till you lay the book aside to leap upon you—that need which is no need, is a demon sucking at the spring of your life. 'No; mine is a reasonable care—an unavoidable care, indeed.' Is it something you have to do this very moment? 'No'. Then you are allowing it to usurp the place of something that is required of you this moment. 'There is nothing required of me at this moment'. Nay, but there is—the greatest thing that can be required of man. 'Pray, what is it?' Trust in the living God. . . . 'I do trust him in spiritual matters.' Everything is an affair of the spirit.[2]

This principle may be harder to follow when our thinking is frightened thinking but it is no less relevant. As long as the fear leads to a sane and honest examining of the dreaded situation in the light of faith and to the decision to act appropriately then the fear is serving its providential purpose which is to act as an alarm signal and stimulate forethought. If such reflection results in the conclusion that no action is necessary or that nothing can at present be usefully done about the matter, the mind should then be detached from the anxiety. This freeing of the mind from irrelevant preoccupation is necessary, not because 'peace of mind' is worth having for its own sake (it certainly is not) but because, while it is evidently not God's will that one should do anything about the feared situation just now, it is bound to be God's will that action should be taken about some other duty or pleasure.

Unless this act of detachment is made we fall into the vague apprehensiveness that never comes to decisions and drowns us in a sea of useless anxiety. Any theology of sanctity must con-

[1] The importance for Christian praying of the thought of the 'sacrament of the present moment' is fully worked out by de Caussade in his *Abandonment to Divine Providence*.

[2] George Macdonald, *An Anthology*, ed. C. S. Lewis, no. 78.

sider such misuse of the fear-reaction just as sinful as the misuse of any other of our vitalities.

Of the many particular fears that produce their relative wants the fear of disapproval deserves consideration. It is clear that most people want to be able to approve of themselves to some extent; they want a reasonable amount of the approval of others; they would like, if they could, to be in the clear with God. Much of this is reasonable wanting, but in a highly competitive and envious culture like that of the western world it becomes exaggerated.

Consequently, many people who make no provision for thinking about the way they are living life, do not notice how perfectionist their private attitude to themselves has become, do not realize how they tend never to be satisfied with their handling of any given task or encounter. They are always comparing their performance with what they might have done or what they think other people would have done in the same situation. The resulting inner monologue of self-depreciation may sometimes look like humility but is really spiritual pride. It is set in motion by the assumption that there is a point of adequate performance at which one *would* approve of oneself, that one ought to have reached this, and by (generally unconscious) anger at not reaching it. St. Francis de Sales referred to these thoughts as 'proud humilities'.

> Cast off all these injured, unquiet and angered and consequently proud humilities; learn to tolerate yourselves patiently ... practise gentleness towards yourselves, as towards others, reproving yourselves without anger, bitterness or spite.[1]

Next door to this unreal dream of self-approval is our desire for other people's approval and the fear of not securing it. We may be anxious about our work, or our children, or some other area of life, but continually we find that our desire for the good of others is inextricably mixed up with anxiety about ourselves and the sort of figure we cut in this public world. It is practically impossible to be anxious about one's children (their success, their moral progress) without self-concern. They are, in one sense, extensions of ourselves, and if they go down in the eyes of the world, we go down too.

[1] De Caussade, *On Prayer*, p. 170.

These anxieties would not descend on us if we did not so keenly fear the disapproval of others. It would be good if we could be freed from all this range of fear and compensatory desire.

The freedom comes through a certain Christian common sense. It is the case that none of us can guarantee personal success in any matter. On many occasions we shall fail to impress anyone, fail to do as well in fact as we could. Occasionally we shall fail to the point of being disgraced.

The disgrace is met by Christian thought about forgiveness. The lack of success is a less important affair but it can be prepared for by a concept of legitimate satisfaction.

While it is true that no one can ever say of anything that he has done that it is perfect or anywhere near it, nevertheless it is a sign of spiritual disease never to be satisfied with anything one has done. The Christian is aware of his limitations and sins; but he knows that God can and does work through weak and sinful men (there is no other sort for him to work through). He is aware that at times he will be disgraced, but he knows that after every failure God's forgiveness closes the issue and brings back spiritual confidence and readiness for life again. He can and should be able to end each day with a sense of peace and satisfaction. It is, of course, a religious peace and satisfaction; its main ingredient is the received forgiveness of sins.

The other principal range of fear is fear of disaster, or what the self regards as disaster. These are two very different things, so that this fear ranges from fear of comparatively small changes in the structure of one's life to fear of losing one's job, health, friend, wife, husband, and on to fear of death and the questions that may be asked after it.

The only thing that can deal with this paralysing sense of inadequacy in the face of future possibilities is faith. This faith is not so much a matter of thinking of that imaginary black day and persuading oneself that God would be at hand to defend. It is more a matter of abandoning the limitless potentiality of the future entirely to God. God's will is something we are to do *now*. Therefore, it is not his will that we should play morbid games with unborn time, trying to feel the weight of burdens not yet laid on us and perhaps never to be laid on us. God helps us to do his will now. That is sufficient. Tomorrow is not our concern.

In twenty-four hours tomorrow will be now. When it is now he will be present with his presence, signifying his will and offering grace, but not before.

> Christ is our bread. We can only ask to have him now. Actually he is always there at the door of our souls, wanting to enter in, though he does not force our consent. If we agree to his entry, he enters; directly we cease to want him, he is gone. We cannot bind our will today for tomorrow, we cannot make a pact with him that tomorrow he will be within us, even in spite of ourselves. Our consent to his presence is the same as his presence. Consent is an act, it can only be actual, that is to say, in the present. We have not been given a will which can be applied to the future. Everything which is not effective in our will is imaginary.[1]

It is the same with the most unnerving tomorrow that faces us:

> I have a sinne of fear, that when I have spunne
> My last thred, I shall perish on the shore;
> Sweare by thyself, that at my death thy sonne
> Shall shine as he shines now, and heretofore;[2]

It is probable that this particular fear is a peculiarly Christian one and will not disturb so much people who do not think in the Christian tradition. Certainly it seems that the more listless and enervated one is the more one looks forward to death. But the thought of ceasing to exist terrifies or at least revolts people who love this life to the full, even though logically there is nothing to fear from nothingness. Accordingly, this fear is found, exquisitely expressed often, in the classical hedonism, and ruefully in modern forms of this (in the work of Camus and Simone de Beauvoir for example), and in the true humanism of Christianity. And when Christianity adds to this thought of 'losing, though full of pain, this intellectual being'[3] the prospect of not reaching joys that have been promised so long and imagined so desirably, this is just about the last twist of the knife.

In this realm of mystery and fear Christian believers recall a kind of promise, much relied on, never completely disproved: 'Lo I am with you always, even to the end of the world.' It is

---

[1] Simone Weil, *Waiting on God* (Routledge and Kegan Paul, 1951), p. 148.
[2] John Donne, *A Hymne to God the Father*.
[3] John Milton, *Paradise Lost*, Book 2. 146.

open now to any believer to find this promise being honoured. It is not open to anyone *now* to hear Jesus calling to him in the hour of his death, bidding him come to him, as it is recorded he once shouted to Simon Peter to come and not fear the wind in his face. But because he is always with us *now*, our faith is that when that momentous Then is now for us, it will be his presence.

There is another fear which normally is not seen as fear because from the front it looks just like ordinary discouragement, but when you go round behind it, you see that it is really a kind of fear. It is the fear of holiness.

Jacques Rivière, reading St. Teresa, makes this comment:[1]

> Fear of the abyss. Fear of this frightful interlacing of demands into which one falls as soon as one consents to God. I tremble lest the patience I may have shown in the trials God has given me to bear so far should encourage him to give me new ones, greater ones. . . . I am not made for such things. . . . I am too much in step with life. My God, keep away from me the temptation of sanctity. . . . It is not my work. Don't be mistaken. I am not that sort of man.

There is no point in denying that we both want to belong to God and are afraid of all this entails. The point is made in a different way by Henri de Lubac:[2]

> The fear of prayer; is this fear of illusion or of the truth? Fear of difficulties in one's mental life or fear of God? And isn't it perhaps fear of finding oneself and fear of losing oneself?

[1] Jacques Rivière, *À la trace de Dieu* (Gallimard), pp. 243–4.
[2] Henri de Lubac, *Paradoxes* (Editions du Seuil), p. 152.

73

8

Suffering

IT is part of the Christian way of living life that one must
expect sufferings of one kind and another which derive entirely from the fact that one is attempting to live in the
Christian way. There will be points of conflict with the life of the
contemporary world both in its conventional purposelessness
and disorder and, of course particularly, when and where it is
organized in an anti-Christian form.

This form of suffering has traditionally had, in the Christian
view, an aura of honour and solemnity. It is suffering *par excellence*. The mind can relate it to the cross of Jesus without self-
indulgence or blasphemy. His cross was the climax of all the
misunderstanding and hostility that he incurred from choosing
what he thought was the will of God for him. So that it is
essential to the profound and universal image of the cross in
Christian spirituality that it is suffering you would have avoided
if you had chosen another way of life and from which you can
easily release yourself by now choosing another way of life.

It is not legitimate to call some unavoidable physical dis-
ability your 'cross', like, say, your arthritis or asthma or deafness
or that your hair is always dry and unmanageable. The cross is
not erected in the realm of necessity; it does not mean unavoidable pain. It is the suffering that comes to you from following
Christ and seeking 'in his name' to do the will of God.

This is not suffering, therefore, from which we can honestly
seek to be released. We can only pray 'Lead us not into temptation but deliver us from evil'; which means, surely, that we are
expressing our (fearful) wish that life may not bring us into
situations in which we shall lose our faith or deny what we think
to be God or refuse to do what we see to be his will, but that if
we do come into situations in which these are possibilities (as of
course we shall) we may have the grace to win through, we may
be delivered from the evil of life there.

But most of our sufferings in the western world are of the other kind, the kind that is common to all men and comes from the realm of necessity, from the evil of life.

There is much misunderstanding about this suffering. It is not true that all pain is evil. Pain has been described (I think by Sherington) as the physical adjunct of a protective reflex. The operative word in that definition is the word 'protective'. Within our human being is installed a set of alarm signals. When we put our hand in the bath water to test the temperature and feel a sharp sting of pain, it is not justifiable to call that 'evil' or dignify it with the word 'suffering'. What has happened is that we have been warned that, had we blithely stepped into the bath believing that all is for the best, we would have been severely blistered. Such pain is part of a world of protective reflexes which, to the Christian, is part of the providential care.

No one doubts the usefulness of this built-in neurological warning system, nor its marvellous complexity or its reliability. It is one of the principal guides and allies of life. A considerable amount of the pain and discomfort of *normal* illness is related to it. And such pain does not deserve deep sympathy as though it were calamity, and it ought not to get it.

It is when pain *exceeds* its protective function, when it is more than mere warning, when it is so persistent and intense that it indicates serious physical disorder or creates great distress in the sufferer, it is then that it justifiably excites sympathy and concern. It is then that steps are taken to relieve it, by medical care, by drugs, if necessary by surgery.

Of course the problem of pain is more complicated than this. The threshold of sensitiveness to pain varies from individual to individual and according to many factors. But one factor is mental attitude—for example, one's general view of life, and the degree to which one has grown up to expect external help when things are not going as they should. The dependent person's tolerance of pain will always be less than that of the independent personality.

And pain is not only physical. There is such a thing as mental and emotional pain. Initially this has the same protective purpose. The tension, the reduction of interest in life and enjoyment of life, the inability to concentrate on one's work, which are characteristic symptoms of anxiety, cannot be called evil, though they are extremely painful. They are warnings, signals to the self that some issue of personal life is crying out for decision and solution. If we are in normal health we heed such warnings and attend to the problem. Many such anxiety situations are not rightly regarded as suffering; they are part of the normal growth of the self, which matures through a continuing process of willed change and adaptation.

It is when such pain exceeds its purpose, fails to stimulate us to necessary action, and intensifies and accumulates and dominates the mind and brings us to a psychological standstill, it is then that we have truly entered the realm of suffering. Many people in our day know the lonely horror of this tract of human experience.

A similar distinction has to be made in the subject of death itself. It is true that there is a strand of revolt in the biblical attitude to mortality, there is a deep sense of death as *the* enemy, but there is also a strand of acceptance of the conditions of human existence, there is an awareness of the normality of death. It is part of normal life that somewhere round the age of 70 or 80 the body comes to the climax of a process of retarding and deterioration that has been going on much longer than we realize as a result of which it ceases to function. This is part of the way things are. It is tragic for people with no faith but not for the Christian. For the Christian there is natural grief at separation from someone deeply loved, natural depression at any humiliating or painful features of this particular death, and natural anxiety over domestic difficulties caused by it; but normal death is not *tragic* for the mature Christian believer. It is the appointed means of leaving this life and entering the next.

Abnormal death is another matter altogether. Death that comes abnormally early or suddenly or violently or in association with some form of life's evil plunges all involved into experience that is truly described as suffering.

It is part of Christian realism to distinguish between on the one hand the normal pains that are incurred in the process of personal growth and adaptation to life or are examples of the many signals and warnings by which we are protected and, on the other hand, the sufferings that are the result of the disorder and evil of life. Normal pain requires from us common sense, understanding and appropriate action. Suffering can be adequately sustained only by faith.

The believer who is seeking God and God's meaning in his suffering should attempt to put his suffering in the right category. Is what I am going through part of the normal pain that accompanies the growth and fulfilment of the self, so that what is required of me primarily is understanding of the situation and appropriate decision? Or is it a major experience of adversity in which I need to draw on the deepest spiritual assurances and convictions I have?

If it is real suffering, two steps at least are clear for the praying Christian. He needs to accept the situation, reject his resentment and self-pity, and receive into his life this unbelievable incarnation of God, because every experience is a form of God's presence. The second step is to wish to do God's will in this situation as in any other. The thought of doing the will of God renders many distinctions void; there is, in the Christian view, essentially no difference between a man of 70 dying of cancer and a man of 20 at the height of his intellectual and physical power deciding his career. Both have an infinite future before them and both can want to do God's will here and now—the patient to endure the restriction and termination of his earthly life in faith and love, the young man to sustain the competition of the many earthly opportunities before him and decide between them in faith and love.

The basic Christian posture would seem to be the same for everyone, young and old, fortunate or unfortunate, and it is decided by the conviction that in God's will is our peace. 'Thy will be done' is wrongly interpreted in a merely backward-looking sense of resignation to what has happened; its full significance is that it is a creative and forward-looking act—'in this situation that has come to me I want to know and do God's will as fully as I can'. The result of adopting this attitude is not that the struggle ceases but that what it is all about changes completely. For the Christian believer, in suffering, the struggle is not 'about' *enduring* the suffering but *serving God in it*.

The doing of God's will is what gives meaning to every situation whether it is happy or revolting. Suffering is given a Christian meaning by being accepted as the sphere in which it is appointed that I serve God at this time.

We may not be able to see what God is doing or going to do with our service, but our faith is that to serve him is the meaning of life and that ultimately this will be clear in a fulfilment of understanding and joy that may well be unimaginable here and now though occasionally people have flashes of conviction here and now that it is the truth.

But normally in great suffering it is not possible to see any good that can ever come out of it. It feels like being in hell or at best an indefensible waste of human experience. It does not look as if Jesus saw what God was doing or would do with what he was suffering. The darkness deepened and he did not feel that the Lord was abiding with him. Indeed he almost died in despair, feeling outrageously deceived, as though all he had done and suffered meant nothing at all and his faith should not have been put in God but in something else if humanity had had the wit to think up an alternative. But at the last minute the pure faith of the man shone out again like the sun struggling round the edge of a cloud.

But even though suffering often seems like a waste of time, the fact is that no time in which God is served is wasted. The service of God is the sanctification of time, and this is true with a particular solemnity of painful and apparently meaningless time.

Exactly how God makes use of our service we can never understand fully and often have no clue at all. We can never understand this fully because what God is doing extends beyond this world of time into eternity, so that even if we think we can see the meaning of some earthly suffering here and now, that certainly does not exhaust its meaning.

The wounds of Jesus *in time* have revealed the love of God to millions of human beings, and indeed go on doing this in the most stupendous spiritual harvest this world has ever seen gathered. But that does not exhaust their meaning, because God's purpose is only finally completed beyond time. What Jesus's sufferings mean beyond time we do not know, but we believe that they have a mysterious and culminating meaning there. This conviction is conveyed in the New Testament image of the risen Christ not completely transformed but carrying the marks of his earthly sufferings still. Some of this thought is carried by one of the Wesley hymns that Methodists today do not seem able to bring themselves to sing.[1] It may be that we have to accept the fact that this kind of imagery does not help us to understand life and God better, or love either of them more.

But when we are presented with suffering that seems to have borne no fruit in time at all, that of the criminal, the dead who went out young, the complete failures who never got into satisfying relationship with anyone and felt outside every joy, the always starving whose existence is a standing reproach to God who has given them life in such an outrageous form, it is time to say that in the Christian understanding of life its meaning is not confined to this life but is developed, purged, clarified, worked out in range upon range of significance the other side of death (which, as Rilke said, is but the side of life that is turned from us).

In this faith there is the conviction that nothing need be wasted and every evil is not finally and forever itself but can and will be made into good.

Christian believers have a singular nervousness about this faith, as though it is something that has lost the respect of the world. In thirty years of pastoral ministry I have seen Christian intellectual perplexity transfer from concepts like the Virgin Birth and the 'existence of God' to the belief in the resurrection of the dead and the life everlasting. These are the problems now apparently. It is impossible to say whether this is a deeply felt concern or just one of the ways twentieth-century people like to play at frightening themselves, a habit Christians have picked up from the company they keep and must of course keep. But our generation certainly has a taste for despair, 'the richest of all the devil's elixirs'.[2] To see life as unrescuably locked in time, to think that everything is ultimately for death, is to live within despair. This capitulation would seem to have been made too easily.

Certainly human beings have to live with mystery, whatever the conceptual scheme by which they attempt to interpret their brief lives. It is just as much a mystery that the truth about life should be uncongenial to humanity (as the death merchants think it is) as is the Christian idea that it is in the long run friendly. And in each case it is a matter of faith; and each is

---

[1] Charles Wesley, 'Arise my soul arise', *Methodist Hymn Book*, 368.
[2] Georges Bernanos, *Diary of a Country Priest* (Fontana Books), p. 95.

worth exploring. But no one *knows*. It is odd that Christians should surrender so much with such little reason.

The Christian faith makes possible an attitude to suffering in virtue of which it is not wasted experience and useless pain, but a giver of life.[1] This attitude is one of faith that God comes in the situation both as asker and giver (giver of what he asks), that the situation therefore can be and should be realistically accepted, and that what is to be done 'about' it is the doing of God's will *in* it.

Again and again we are faced with situations in which in some sense life is testing us with the challenge to give or give up something valuable, even precious, even absolutely necessary to us. Sometimes we can side-step the sacrifice asked of us; but then we inevitably lose, though this may not become immediately obvious to us. We shall do all our thinking in that region less efficiently, more evasively, after this refusal to face things. On the other hand we can accept the situation and go through with it, even though 'it' is catastrophe. Then we immediately gain in honesty and strength and our sense of reality, even if we cannot for the time being answer the questions the ghastly situation raises. And, much more importantly, again and again it is found that something that the situation requires is provided, that we are given the power to give what it appears we are asked to give. In this sense when dark experience approaches it is normally the case, on this view, that the only way out is the way further in. All experience refused is a true waste of time; and there follows an impoverishment of the personality, which becomes bitter, self-centred, backward-looking, resenting life, indeed the most boring condition into which anyone can degenerate. But when experience is lived through without regrets and reservations, lived through with the whole of one's being, it is found that what looked unendurable, as it appeared on the horizon of possibility, proves itself quite a different thing, as though someone shares the load when the moment comes for taking it on. Readiness for experience gives people access to a new level of life on which what they suffer is absorbed in a much deeper range of feeling and understanding. What looked, as it was approached, as the place of sacrifice, turns out to be the

[1] When Baudelaire spoke of 'la fertilisante douleur' he spoke with Christian understanding. Cf. *Fleurs du Mal*, ed. Edith Starkie, p. xvii.

place where it is found that the Lord provides, the truth about God being that he is not a taker but a giver.

This point of view emerges slowly through the Bible, though there are moments when it shines out with great clarity, in a sense before its time in the stories of the sacrifice of Isaac and of Jacob's wrestling with his nameless angel, and then in the temptations and passion of Christ. It has a culminating beauty in the account of the conversation on the Emmaus Road.

The disciples on the road to Emmaus see Jesus only as an ordinary man, someone who is of no special significance for the solution of the problems that perplex them. But when their minds have been fully stretched in the examination of their religious tradition, its ideas about God, life, pain and death, they come to a kind of relaxation of the mind, a moment when things at last fall into place and they understand.

The moment when this long process of thought reaches its fulfilment and they *see* is when he takes the bread, gives thanks, breaks it and gives to them. It is not possible to detail all the thoughts that helped to make the light of that moment. But there is one that is clear. It is that the line of God's purpose connects offering, thanking, being broken and sharing with the glory of God, and that if you look back not only through the history of the Jews but through the whole journey of humanity, you will find again and again that this has been so.

These thoughts make a sense of life, put a meaning into life; but whether it is what life in fact means no one can prove, it is a matter of faith. This is what Christians believe. These thoughts have made sense of life for a great number of people and continue to do so. They do this not by putting an end to further questions—the questioning will never be done—but by ending the kind of mental blockage and resistance and unproductiveness suggested by the idea in the Emmaus story that their eyes were *held* so that they *could not* recognize him.

There are certain ways of thinking which do in fact hold the mind, clamp it down in resentment or sheer perplexity. And there are ways of thinking with which you can live and work, which seem to enlighten the mind, are worth exploring, and enable the self to go forward and to want to go forward into more human experience.

And one of these is the great nexus of thought from the Bible which connects so closely the offering of the self, thankfulness, suffering and sharing with the ultimate glory and fulfilment of life.

The sum of it all is that in the Christian view all the time, in both pleasant and hideous experience, there is only one truly valid prayer, that we should be given the desire and the ability to do what we understand to be God's will in the present situation.

It is true that western Christianity has made too much of the sufferings of Christ, it has used too frequently the crucifix as a principal visual aid to prayer. One of the benefits of twentieth-century ecumenism is the west's increasing interest in Orthodoxy whose joyful concentration on the risen and glorified Christ will undoubtedly change, is changing the obsession with pain in western spirituality. When this fault has been corrected we shall be able to see the truth without sentimentality or morbidity that in the Christian way of praying the consecration of pain has in fact a very special place.

In suffering it is hard to be objective enough to want to do God's will, so that suffering is that experience *par excellence* that both tests faith and enables faith to prove itself. And Christians have found again and again that when suffering is lived through without resentment, as an experience in which God particularly, nervously, hopefully asks us to do his will, it becomes unexpectedly fruitful, it makes new life. It is of course not always so. Sometimes suffering destroys faith, destroys the whole self, and not one hopeful word can be said about it. But there is so much of the other evidence that Christians will always argue that, handled by faith, suffering has a special relation to the presence of God in the world.

Until we have some knowledge of this depth in the Christian way of experiencing life we shall find it extremely hard to believe the teaching it has produced, and we shall continue our subterfuges and evasions, our futile playing with experience on the border of the only realm in which we may conceivably find peace and power.

But, once we have proved this Christian truth in experience, we shall know that even in pain the only prayer that is worth praying is the Gethsemane prayer of Jesus. This kind of prayer is honest: it does not pretend a bravery or faith it does not possess.

It is ready to admit into consciousness whatever lurks below the surface of the mind. But it moves forward, not easily but successfully, through fear and honesty, to the single desire that in whatever one must go through now one will have the power and discernment to do the will of God.[1]

This characteristic Christian attitude to life is set forth whenever the Eucharist is celebrated—the sacrament in which all is offered to God, to be taken out of our dream or terror and made part of his kingdom. And it is just the case that a fantastic number of Christians have prayed in this way down the centuries of the human experiment. They have taken the particular gloom or sorrow or fear into which life has plunged them and gone to some place where the Church was doing the Eucharist. There, in the setting forth of the only truly offered being that ever lived, they have tried to offer up this situation (whatever it was) that terrified them or made them furious with God. They have tried to separate *themselves* from it, to offer up not only it but their ridiculous wishes concerning it or their desire to escape from it. They have sought to see it within the purpose of God, within the great image of that purpose truly fulfilled in a human life which is the sacrifice of Christ. They have been ready to bring their particular pain into vital relation with all that God wills for man, all that they have believed through Christ about God's ways of working with man and through man. And again and again the certain grace has come. Their desires and fears have changed out of all recognition, and have become first an acceptance, then a wish to do what the situation requires rather than to be relieved of its burden, a wish to make their distress a creative part of God's presence in life, and finally a fresh appetite for their difficult world.

---

[1] Cf. D. Z. Phillips, *The Concept of Prayer*, pp. 129–30. 'Praying to a God for whom all things are possible is to love God in *whatever* is the case.'

9

Desiring Other People's Good

WHEN the Christian believer prays for others he is penetrating even further into the realm of self-offering. He is not to be thought of as, in a stationary position, signalling requests to some being 'out there' to help some third person in some other stationary position (though one of pain) in our marvellous universe.

> I hurried and, having told Penny to pray, prayed *Let him live, let him live, do not let my father be sick.* The prayer was addressed to all who would listen; in concentric circles it widened, first, into the town, and, beyond, into the hemisphere of sky, and, beyond that, into what was beyond. The sky . . . was still deep daylight blue. . . . If the blue dome beyond the town was an illusion, how much more, then, of an illusion might be what is beyond that. *Please*, I added to my prayer, like a reminded child.[1]

In contrast to that wistful, but conventional, concept of prayer, in the Christian view prayer is principally the means which believers use to maintain their relationship with God, their responsiveness to his will for them, their particular understanding of life in terms of his revelation in Christ.

When any individual is in this right relation to God he contributes to making the whole universe, in which his friends also have their, maybe painful, being, that much more 'right', fulfilled (as Christians have been taught to imagine plenitude), mobile, sensitive to the divine action. When only one person is in right relation to God, the whole universe, as it affects mankind, is nearer its divine intention, and that much (of course, quite immeasurably) more receptive of the redemptive presence of God.

Prayer does not look like this to most people. It looks as if it is a means of persuading God to act in the world. This view of

[1] John Updike, *The Centaur* (Penguin Books), p. 114.

prayer is guaranteed to make the religious life extremely difficult for thinking people and ultimately insupportable. People
who adopt it will not be long before they are thinking of God
as a power to be used. It is likely that they are then out of the
world of Christian faith and in the world of magic.

If prayer is regarded simply, without qualification, as a request to God to do certain things he would not do if we did not
ask him and will do simply because we ask him, we are wasting
our time. If we are simply wanting something done in a certain
situation we ought ourselves, no doubt in faith, to be doing
something to support the creative agencies relevant to the subject of our concern. There is no reason to think that God will do
on his own what he purposes to do *with man*. If man will not end
war, then, though we pray forever, God will not end it *for man*.

Accordingly when we pray for the peace of the world, we do
not pray in order to inform God about some area where war is
threatened or raging, nor to give him information about our
own anxieties. He knows both, better than we. Nor do we pray
in order to persuade him to take the nobility and agony of
human freedom and responsibility from us and intervene in
some set of circumstances to alter them. We pray in order to
express, in a context of Christian faith and worship, our com-
passion for humanity and our anxiety about its present and
future fortunes together with our continuing trust in God. We
hold together, in the presence of God, the situation that dismays
us and our nevertheless still trusting minds. We do this because
this is the way Christian love functions, whether the individual
praying Christian understands it theologically or not. We do it
because we believe this relationship of candour and trust in
relation to God is what he desires and is strengthened by this
kind of expression, and because we believe that God instructs
minds so disposed and acts through them for the fulfilling of his
purpose.

Many Christian believers may find such description of intercession quite inadequate. Certainly all attempts at describing
the mystery of prayer must be inadequate. But the inadequacy
of the conventional expectations associated with intercessory
prayer and of much use of it in the life of the Church also needs
critical comment. One thinks of all the pious talk about answers
to prayer, the sermon illustrations of the effectiveness of prayer

in critical situations, the arranging of days of national prayer in times of public anxiety. All of this (even if defensible in specific instances) inevitably encourages people to think of prayer as specially related to crisis, and of answers to prayer as specially related to the fulfilment of our wishes.

Christian spirituality has never related prayer specially to crisis, and not at all to the fulfilment of our wishes, with the inescapable twist of self-concern with which they form in the mind. The principal idea all along has been that prayer is to be understood as the means of nourishing our day-to-day religious life so that we shall be able to do some part at any rate of what God wishes, his wishes being thought to be far more closely related to the glory of life than ours are.

It is, accordingly, much to be regretted that petition and intercession are for so many people the principal, often the only, forms of prayer. They are extremely difficult forms of prayer, requiring constant scrutiny, because they are so liable to degenerate into forms of panic and materialism.

When someone we deeply love is in special need which we are apparently unable to help, the more we realize that prayer is the only channel of activity left us, and the more earnestly we want to help this person, the more doubts begin to nag at the mind. What claim have I on God's great storehouse of power? What right have I to assume that God wishes to use his power in the way suggested by the prayer that is even now forming in my mind? And suppose there is some relation between God's available power and the obedience of his children? There is a tradition that the prayer of a righteous man availeth much, but I have obeyed so little, blasphemed so much, drifted along with God a merely marginal consideration in this or that passage of fear through which I have at intervals lived. What if only those who have put something into the Bank of Grace can assume that their cheques drawn on it will be honoured?

The more one thinks on these lines the more gloom descends. But it is not a useless gloom, because it suggests that this way of thinking about prayer cannot be right. It cannot be right because it must necessarily lead either to pride or to despair. I must conclude that God will certainly hear my prayer, or that he will certainly not.

The mistake is the familiar one of thinking of God as someone to be persuaded to help, a source of power to be brought into a situation from which he is assumed to be excluded until he is brought in by prayer. This is a form of attempting to use God, and is no part of the Christian use of praying.

The Christian idea of intercession is that it is not a means we employ to persuade God to act in a situation he has presumably overlooked or into which he needs to be summoned, but a means God employs to summon *our* help through our membership in the Body of Christ.

'If you abide in me, and my words abide in you, ask whatever you will, and it shall be done for you' (John xv. 7, R.S.V.). The guarantee of the effectiveness of the asking resides in the fact that he who asks is 'in Christ' and will therefore not ask the nonsense and infantile dream of uninstructed human asking, but only 'in His name'. Truly Christian prayer is part of the eternal prayer and sacrifice of the great High Priest. Our prayer is Christian prayer as we enter into the self-offering of Christ, as we want to be part of God's purpose and channels through which his love can act.

Accordingly, when we pray for someone who is in great trouble, it is quite legitimate to ask for him to be delivered from the evil in his situation. We are expressing our natural desire that he should be given a 'happy issue' out of all his afflictions, but we are not trying to persuade God to do anything about the situation other than bring in his kingdom there (and this he does not need to be persuaded to do). We are expressing the natural desires of natural human love within the context of our faith in God. Faith means that we are prepared for things to go any way, better or worse as we understand these terms, and that in either case we wish that this person will continue to serve God and that we ourselves shall too, and that we believe that all of us whether we live or die are the Lord's.

God is not a human being who gets up from place A and goes to place B and does something because he has been asked. He just *is present*, and as love, through people who are in right relationship with him; and through them he does more than we ask or think.

It is only in the Eucharist, the central and representative act of Christian prayer, that praying for the good of others can be understood in the Christian way. In the Anglican and Methodist rite the great intercession comes immediately after the Offertory. It is rightly argued that this arrangement is a disadvantage in that Offertory and Consecration are separated by too great a gap,[1] and all revisions of the liturgy are correcting this. But the old arrangement does enable people to see that offering and intercession are inseparably involved in each other. We customarily think that it is insufficient to offer God anything without ourselves; indeed, on the Christian view, it is sin to offer God everything *but* ourselves. And there is a deep piety in regarding the Offertory as an offering of not only our alms and oblations but also of our whole lives for God's use. This point will not be obscured by rearrangements of the order of Offertory and Great Intercession in the revisions of the liturgy now being prepared. The Eucharist is a great drama of thanking and offering, and all Christian petition and intercession cannot be understood correctly unless they are seen as within that great action.

It is only when we stand with God and his redemptive purpose, at any rate in desire and intention, that we can think of the needs of the Church and the world 'in His name', as God thinks of them.

Our thinking of the needs of men makes us want God's mercy to be brought to them in the glooms of need and hope in which they wait. But in the Christian view the great bearer of God's merciful action is none other than the Body of Christ. God chooses to spread the victory of the cross through the world by means of all who are united to Christ in his Church, among whom of course are we ourselves. Therefore to ask 'in Christ' that God's will be done in the world involves *at the same time* offering ourselves to God to be truly part of that through which he intends to answer prayer for the world's salvation. This is what it means to pray that we 'may be partakers of his most blessed Body and Blood'.

Every Christian prayer for others involves the realization that he who prays is inextricably bound up with the answer. His prayer is not a mere message sent to God, voicing a request. It carries him with it deep into all that costly action which is the purpose of God in the life of the world. If it is not this it is simply the crying of a child.

[1] Gregory Dix, *The Shape of the Liturgy*, p. 692.

Each time you take a human soul with you into your prayer, you accept from God a piece of spiritual work with all its implications and with all its cost—a cost which may mean for you spiritual exhaustion and darkness, and may even include vicarious suffering, the Cross. In offering yourselves on such levels of prayer for the sake of others, you are offering to take your part in the mysterious activities of the spiritual world; to share the saving work of Christ. . . . Real intercession is not merely a petition but a piece of work, involving perfect, costly self-surrender to God for the work he wants done on other souls.[1]

The prayer that is mere request, without self-offering, is not prayer 'in his name' and is not worth the time it takes to say.

This throws some light on the delays of providence. There must be many problems (the unity of the Church, the peace of the world) whose solution must wait because God intends the answers to our prayers for these matters to come through persons willing to be bearers of the answer. To bring the world before God in prayer is to stand where you can hear most clearly the most tragic voice in the universe, God's despair of man, 'Whom shall I send and who will go for us?'

And so, when we pray for someone in the name of Christ, we are standing within God's redemptive purpose and asking that that purpose may reach out to that person and enfold him, and *at the same time* we are affirming our desire that we, if possible, may be used to bear God's mercy to him. We may well be used directly. Among the costliest prayers that can ever be said are the prayers of a husband for his wife, of parents for their children.

But the situation may be one in which we cannot be used in some act of direct service. God will then not be able to use more of us than the love which has driven us to pray, but this love, while being used by him in ways beyond our understanding, can also pass into action in other spheres of life nearer to us (where what *we* do is important) and therefore affect for good that whole in which we and the person we feel we cannot directly serve have our sensitive being.

Even so, one cannot forget this haunting sense of belonging to one another which Christ seemed to want his disciples to feel very deeply. God wills to give himself in answer to our requests

[1] Evelyn Underhill, *Life as Prayer* (Collected Papers), pp. 57–9.

for each other, as well as our requests for ourselves, so that we may belong more closely to one another, in being in some degree responsible for one another. And so we can only surmise, we can never know (until he tells us at the end) how much of the pure air of his kingdom we now breathe because of other people's prayers.

To the Christian believer, the question: What should we pray for when we pray for others? is just another form of the question: What is most worth having in life?

If we are in touch with the source and substance of all good we shall be fools to ask for anything less than this, for anything less than the best.

The best thing in life is the kingdom of God. The best that can happen to anyone, or to the world, is to be filled with all the fullness of God. One cannot stand within the purpose of God, ready to pray in his name, and ask for anything less, or anything else.

The worst that can happen to anyone is to be separated from God, which must indeed be hell, whether it feels like what people call 'hell' or not. Anxiety is justified when it seems that people are falling into hell or are in danger of doing this. Rejoicing is justified when it appears that they are moving towards God or are in his presence and in some degree aware of this, even though they may never attach the word 'God' to that upholding or gladness through which they are passing.

The connection between this basic Christianity and some of the intercessory practice of the Church is not always clear. When there are special prayers about our water supply only when there is a drought, or days of prayer only when war is threatened or in progress, or prayers for people by name in the worship of the Church only in connection with serious illness or bereavement, the truth about the use of praying is much obscured, as also is the truth about calamity. Certainly where there are special groups in the Church devoted to intercession for the sick it should not be automatically assumed that these are truly gathered together 'in his name'.

In the twentieth century, when the odds against personal happiness are so high anyway and most people find that God goes on rather long with hiding himself, it would help if everyone, but particularly believers, inquired of themselves what they imagine evil to be. When we use the prayer 'lead us not into temptation but deliver us from evil' is there some identifiable dread at the back of the mind about which we feel 'whatever happens, save us from that'? While 'that' must inevitably have a different content for different people, Christian believers find their image of it much modified and even transformed as they learn Christ. Part of this transformation is the growing conviction that much physical illness, and certainly normal terminal illness, are by no means such dreadful evils as despair, loss of faith, hatred or fear of life, triviality, the disintegration of a marriage, the loneliness of neurosis.[1] It might be assumed from Christian practice that it is believed that someone who is ill with pneumonia deserves the public prayer of the Church more than these others whose hells are so intensely personal and private. The fact is that much of the true evil of personal life cannot be made the subject of public intercession in any identifiable manner; and this is one of the points in the prayer of the Church where the liturgy needs the completion of private prayer.

Another questionable feature of much current use of intercession is the obsession with number and quantity. The use of vigils among instructed Christians (who cannot be suspected of thinking that they are more likely, by this personal inconvenience, to persuade God to act) must be directed not to God but the Church, or perhaps even the world, as a means of stimulating interest in the cause or causes which figure in the intercessions. This is a misuse of praying, since it is only to God the Holy Trinity that Christian prayer is rightly addressed, and he should be addressed sincerely, not by half the self—the other half concerned about the impression we hope we are making on certain people.

And when it is argued that some Christian project (for example, an evangelistic campaign) will be sure to meet with success because of 'the great backing of prayer' it is receiving throughout the country, there could hardly be a better way of teaching, by implication, an idea of prayer that amounts to misinformation.

Somewhere behind these misunderstandings will generally be found the idea of prayer as a means of enlisting the help of God

[1] Actually, the evil to which the prayer refers is that of some unbearable strain under which one denies all that one rightly believes about God.

in the creation or alteration of external circumstances in some way other than through human beings responding to his love. It is sometimes said that all is put theologically right if we add at the end of our prayer, either vocally or mentally, 'if it be thy will'. This proviso can keep our praying at an infantile level for ever. It is far better to surrender the whole pattern of thought whereby we imagine that when we pray we plug in to some supernatural power that does things apart from offered human beings.

That pattern of thought encourages futile speculation about the 'mechanics' of intercession, for example, that it may all work by telepathy; it creates a whole dimension of approval of God when things go right in our view, just as it creates a range of disappointment with him and accusation against him when things go wrong in our view; and all this has nothing whatever to do with the life of faith.

Christians pray for others because this is part of the Christian way of living and loving. We are attempting to live in what we understand is Christ's way; we desire to be wholly involved in this; and therefore all that, as taught by Christ, we consider important, we want to bring into this Christian attitude to life. We bring the person we love or the cause about which we are concerned into all that Christ has taught us about God and life, into our dependence on God and our desire to serve him. Such love, such concern is consecrated by being so related to the thought of God (and we long for the consecration of life as in winter one longs for the spring). But consecration always modifies. By consecration, the bread and wine in the Eucharist assume an entirely different meaning from that which they normally have. And the consecration of any wish, its being offered to God, will most certainly change its substance. We begin praying by thinking 'this is what I hope for in this situation and I trust God not to let me down'; we end by thinking 'this is how this situation looks in the light of God's purpose, this is what I must now do to serve God in it, and this is what I really want'. And in some situations what we then do will obviously be very important, obviously materially help. But in some other situations, in our helplessness before the intractability and frustration of life, our prayer simply becomes one with that agony that, as Pascal said, Christ will be in to the end of the world.

If we say that we want more from religion than this, more guarantees that it 'works', the fact is that we are in some odd, primitive world and a very long way from home. Home for the Christian is the foot of the cross.

It is worth while spending some time in working out what is the right thing to ask, rather than ask what first comes into our mind and then add this conventional proviso, 'if it be according to thy will'. It is not unintelligent to assume that it is God's will that we should run the risk of experiencing the hardship of drought until we use our technical knowledge and resources to make due provision for that eventuality. Prayers for rain in August begin to look like man asking God for the answer which God wishes to be given through man's wisdom and industry. An Englishman can say that blandly. It is not one of those truths about God that hurt him very much. It is a very different situation for the Christian in India; for him that truth about God's ways of working becomes a charge against God that some day will need to be answered by God. The (to us) excessive cost of some lessons of human experience (for example, the price humanity is having to pay for learning how to construct international peace) is at present a reproach against God which faith maintains will at length become a reason for saying 'he hath done all things well'.

It is important to be aware of the multiple nature of God's will. At any given moment God's will is a complex of many considerations, such as the maintenance of that reliable order of cause and effect which is the condition of scientific and moral progress, the preservation of human freedom, our need to learn our dependence on him and on each other, our need to learn how to pray, and a host of other factors, some of which in our cleverness we think we know, but always we come to the far rim of knowledge and can go no further, can only return to this mixture of ignorance and faith in which humanity has lived all the time.

All these considerations, taken together, mean, for example, that it was God's will (not his wish) that war should be permitted to break out in September 1939 and last six years.

And the presence or absence of Christian prayer in any situation is one of these many factors through which God's will is manifested. The elements of mystery and complexity which any doctrine of providence must recognize do not make intercessory prayer less necessary, but they do mean that we shall be less inclined to specify the divine action we desire. We shall find ourselves increasingly content to do as our Lord has taught us and simply ask that God's kingdom may come and his will be done in the situation about which we are praying. St. John of the Cross points out that we are 'on surer ground' when we simply lift up to God our needy condition than when we ask in detail for the things we think we need.[1]

Some people are dismayed by the thought of the number of people and causes who should have a place in their prayers. The great host of those for whom they have failed to find room in their devout attention stretches out into the imagined distance, each one an accusation. This is an unnecessary perplexity which disperses as we see our intercessions as our participation in the saving action of the Body of Christ. Obviously we cannot embrace the whole world in our thought; but God can. If our prayer is part of the intercession of the great High Priest, whose love spans the universe, we can play our part in it with gladness and seriousness and without agitation.

It is clearly God's will that we bring into our prayers those whose lives he has closely interlocked with ours in the three worlds which constitute most of our life, the worlds of our family, our friendships and our work. We shall also join in the wider intercessions of the liturgical life of the Church.

For the rest, though we do not forbid any name a mention in our prayers, we need not be anxious about the natural limits of the mind's range. The power of prayer is not confined within such limits. If we abide in Christ and our prayer is in his name, all our prayers, actions, sufferings are taken up into the infinite scope of his activity whose sovereign grace to all extends.

In Gerard Manley Hopkins's poem *The Lantern out of Doors* the poet is concerned with the unknown multitudes of people who pass by us, making an impact on us so slight and transitory that we only just sense their existence. Yet they are persons, with needs and pains. It is dismaying that we who want to love the world must so quickly forget them as they disappear from view. It is sad that 'out of sight is out of mind'. But they do not pass out of the farther seeing and deeper caring of Christ:

[1] St. John of the Cross, *Spiritual Canticle*, ii. 8.

94

Christ minds; Christ's interest, what to avow or amend
There, eyes them, heart wants, care haunts, foot follows kind
Their ransom, their rescue, and first, fast, last friend.

It is good to bring into our intercessions the thought of the infinity of the divine care. It is beautifully expressed in the Liturgy of Basil the Great:

> And those whom we, through ignorance or forgetfulness or the number of names, have not remembered, do Thou, O God, remember them, who knowest the age and the name of each one, who knowest each from his mother's womb. For Thou, O God, art the help of the helpless, the hope of the hopeless, the saviour of the tempest-tossed, the harbour of mariners, the physician of the sick. Be Thou thyself all things to all men, who knowest each and his petition and his dwelling and his need.

But we come back, as we must repeatedly do, to our belief that love is the only power through which God's kingdom will come. Accordingly, each individual's unique world of love is the holiest and most responsible area of his life. No doubt it is not wide enough; and one of the most demonstrable results of genuine faith is that our world of love will be widened. But at any time, whether the person who prays is a young convert or a mature Christian, the people he likes and loves are particularly given to *him* to be lifted up to God in intercessory affection.

Prayer lists are often ridiculed as part of the outmoded paraphernalia of religion, with the odour 'quintessence of hassock' about them. But it is not possible to fulfil this part of Christian love without a list, which one keeps close at hand, in Bible or prayer book, of the people who have particularly shaped one's Christian faith, in other ways contributed to one's sense of *la douceur de la vie*, or asked for our prayers because, whether they are in special trouble or not, they just want this form of being loved. The list is merely an aid to memory which fails much more easily and frequently than affection, especially with the old, and serves to bring to us those whom we want to hold in our love and faith for a while because this is part of the Christian way of loving.

It is natural to reserve a special place for those who mean much to us but happen to have died. Faith in the communion of saints is much attenuated in current Protestantism and hardly

gets out of the Creed into life where alone, of course, it can be
any use. Indeed, Protestant Christianity has not very much to
say to any Christian who has been through the crucial experience of seeing the face he loves most in this world recede into the
inaccessible mystery of death. The embarrassed silence we offer
the bereaved (who usually and naturally want very much to
talk about their beloved dead) is outrageous—the stone with
which our scepticism and inadequate sympathy respond to their
request for bread.

It may be that we shall be helped in this matter by cultures
not as atomized as ours, nor as afraid of death. J. V. Taylor's
book, *The Primal Vision*, in the beautiful chapter titled 'The
Tender Bridge', makes one reflect on the superiority of African
sensitiveness to the thought of death.

> Surely the 'tender bridge' that joins the living and the dead in
> Christ is prayer. Mutual intercession is the life-blood of the fellow-
> ship, and what is there in a Christian's death that can possibly
> check its flow? To ask for the prayers of others in this life, and to
> know that they rely on mine, does not show any lack of faith in the
> all-sufficiency of God. Then, in the same faith, let me ask for their
> prayers still, and offer mine for them, even when death has divided
> us. They pray for me, I may believe, with clearer understanding,
> but I for them in ignorance, though still with love. And love, not
> knowledge, is the substance of prayer.[1]

It is not right that this natural expression of Christian love be
confined to confirmed members of the Church. One of the commonest questions asked of ministers in times of bereavement is
how the widow or widower is to think of a husband or wife who
was not a member of the Church or even an attender at its
worship. The answer is simply that death does not kill love; in
some ways it deepens it. Love wants to express itself, must express itself still. And Christian loving can express itself, without
inhibition, in prayer and faith.

> The words, 'In Adam all . . .' included the whole family of Man
> in death; the promise, 'In Christ all . . .' cannot include less than
> that in life. The genealogies in the Gospel linking Christ himself
> with the unnumbered myriads of the dead are a symbol of the un-
> broken cord with which God will finally draw Adam back to
> Paradise. The Christian's link with his . . . ancestors, in remem-

J. V. Taylor, *The Primal Vision*, p. 168.

brance and unceasing intercession, may be part of that ultimate redemption; for, as Césaire the Martiniquean poet puts it 'there is room for all of us at the rendezvous of victory'.[1]

Once again it is in the Eucharist that this use of praying is given characteristically Christian form. The sacraments are like poetry to theology's prose; they give the essence, the complexity, the mystery of Christian faith in a concentrated immediacy which theology needs volumes to expound. In the Eucharist the Sanctus is said in a positively excited conviction that in prayer distance, death and time are completely transcended, we share in *all* the supernatural life of the whole Body, immersed in the one great stream of grace which God uses to refresh and cleanse and invigorate us as we seek to serve him in the world of distance, death and time.

And it has been part of Christian praying from earliest times to relate this point in Holy Communion especially with vanished smiles and household voices gone, so that it is a moment of great intensity at which public liturgy and the most private prayer can meet and blend. Both the living and the dying depend on this. St. Augustine tells how, at his mother's deathbed

> my brother said something to the effect that he would be happier if she were to die in her own land and not in a strange country. But as she heard this she looked at him anxiously, restraining him with her eye because he savoured of earthly things, and then she looked at me and said: 'See the way he talks'. And then she said to us both: 'Lay this body wherever it may be. Let no care of it disturb you: this only I ask of you, that you should remember me at the altar of the Lord wherever you may be'.[2]

[1] J. V. Taylor, *The Primal Vision*, p. 171.
[2] St. Augustine, *Confessions* (trans. F. J. Sheed), Book ix, 11.

10

Answers

T HE idea of 'answers to prayer' is much more of a nuisance than a help in the life of faith. Its general use among Christian believers suggests that they tend to think of prayer primarily as asking for certain things, the 'answer' being the receiving of these desired results. It is significant that people rarely say that *not* receiving what they wanted was 'an answer to prayer'. Yet any truly religious person, knowing the regressive and irresponsible nature of much of his desiring, and realizing his helplessness before some of his more imperious wants, must often want to give thanks that his desires have not been met.

If the idea of 'answers to prayer' is being employed in order to show that there is 'something in religion' or 'that God exists', it is even more unsatisfactory. The argument 'I prayed to God that my child might not die and he heard my prayer because my child recovered' is perfectly acceptable in the world of faith and human terror. In the world of philosophy it is ludicrous. There is no future for the process of extracting the experience of prayer from the world of religion and setting it in the world of empirical verification. 'One can accept religion in its own terms or reject it; there is no way of justifying it by translating it into other terms.'[1] It is of course possible, for what it is worth, to show that a man's life is consistent with his faith and his prayers. But this, though it has importance in the world of religion, is of little value in the realm of philosophical argument; the life of a schizophrenic is also consistent with his conviction that he hears voices, but this fact has no bearing on the question of the origin of the voices.

There is no 'answer' required to an act of adoration or thanksgiving; such an act is made in faith that it is pleasing to God and is accepted. The proper answer to confession is the assurance of forgiveness, and this comes as satisfactorily in the form of sacra-

[1] *Metaphysical Beliefs*, Toulmin, Hepburn and Macintyre, p. 202.

mental absolution (or the deferment of it) as in any other way one can think of it coming. The answer to petition and intercession, since these are essentially the offering of ourselves and our desires to God to become part of his redemptive work in the world, is to believe ourselves accepted and put to work and to see many of these desires in an entirely new light.

The answer to prayer that matters most is the general result which prayer is expected and intended to achieve, the purpose for which prayer is used; and this is the expression and deepening of our faith in God, our desire for the coming of his rule in our perplexing world, and our love for him and his created world of infinitely interesting persons and things. If prayer does not do this for us, after a reasonable trial, it is a waste of time and should be abandoned for more fruitful activities. Life is just too short to waste time praying if praying does not help one to love life and enjoy it more.

An important part of Jesus's teaching on prayer was the way he so closely associated asking and receiving. Asking and receiving are apparently two parts of the same thing.[1] We are to pray believing that we are in fact receiving that for which we are praying. If we take the Lord's Prayer as the standard, we find that we cannot ask for those things sincerely without beginning at the same time to receive them. We cannot sincerely ask that God's name be hallowed, that he be regarded as the ultimately holy, that the coming of his authority into men's lives be seen as the meaning of existence, without this beginning to happen or increasing its power in us. To ask for God in prayer is to have him then. The answer comes as the words are uttered.

There is no such thing as unanswered prayer if it is truly Christian prayer. We can ask God for all sorts of things that he cannot give—that he should cancel something we did yesterday of which we are now ashamed, or that he will keep some part of the probable future from us. But if we do this we are not asking 'in his name'. When we are 'in Christ' we know that the past cannot be cancelled, it can only be forgiven, which is far better than any cancellation, and the future cannot be avoided but it can be lived through with God. Of course, some of the things we may be inclined to ask for cannot be immediately

[1] Mark xi. 24.

answered in completion, but the answer is being given, is in process of being given. Prayers for the peace of the world are *being answered*—through the disarmament meetings at Geneva, the deliberations at the United Nations Organization in New York, the feeble support of United Nations Associations all over the world, and the struggle each one of us has in his lazy mind to conquer one prejudice, revise one conventional judgment, make any attempt to understand and control his aggressiveness. There is no such thing as unanswered Christian prayer. But because God works his will through persons, the answers wait on the availability of persons willing to carry them. There are always *some* people ready to be vehicles of God's purpose, but sometimes we all sink into despair because, as Jesus put it, the labourers are so few for the harvest of God's inscrutable love, and among these few we so rarely see ourselves.

Asking with the mind of Christ must involve the expectation that the answer will be in terms of that which we believe Christ continually sought for himself and spent his life offering to others, that is to say, the possibility of faith in God, obedience to his will and joy in his presence. This is what praying is 'for'. It is not necessary to force our un-Christian wantings into this mould. It is right that we should be ourselves before God and say simply what we want, not what we think we ought to want. God requires the truth from us even if the truth is that we prefer other things to him.[1] But the honest Christian, in expressing naturally and without inhibition the truth of his own desires, must also be ready to receive the truth about the life of desire as Christianity understands it, which is that God has nothing whatever to give anyone but himself, some share in what he is taking such a long time doing with man, the strain of the infinity of questions his action in the world raises, and a much-attested deposit of love, joy, and peace in the mind.

It may be more significant to speak of the completion or fulfilment, or at least continuation, of prayer instead of attempting to extricate this deep part of Christian living from the problems created by the term 'answered prayer'. A prayer is not an event that can be isolated from the life of a believer and shown to have a beginning and an end; it is not a transaction; it is not a request granted or ungranted.

[1] Cf. J. Burnaby, *Soundings* (ed. Vidler), pp. 234-5.

This is not to say that prayer is merely subjective, an inward event in the psychological life of a believer. Sighs, exclamations and cheers are not prayers, though they are the 'thin end of the wedge' of prayer, they are the beginning of mental processes infinitely important in the spiritual life (sorrow, wonder, approval) and they help to show how basically natural prayer is. Everyone sighs, exclaims, approves. In Christian prayer the ability to experience life in these ways is educated and ordered and given the opportunity of proper expression within a religious tradition of what is considered the proper subject of grief and wonder and approval. This is part of that purification and transformation of desire which we have already seen prayer to be.

In the Beatitudes,[1] which passage of scripture is the oddest catalogue of happiness that must ever have occurred to man, Jesus takes some characteristic situations of conflict and despair in his day and says, in effect, that he knows a way of thinking about life in virtue of which we would no longer worry or rage about being in such situations, would not long above all things to escape from them. And this because, if we took up with Jesus and learned his way of seeing life, we would want other things more—the doing of God's will on earth, living as 'a child of God', the sight of righteousness displacing unrighteousness, and the vision of the glory of God. These new wants would not make us inactive in this world. They would indeed add energy to our work to improve the situation and remove the evil in it. But they would take the resentment out of our struggle and give us perseverance and zest for it all.

It is in this way that, instead of speaking about prayer 'being answered', it is more suitable to think of prayer simply as part of the on-going life of faith. One of the results of prayer is that the Christian way of living life becomes more possible and more interesting. This new situation is itself mobile and vital, and it will be the scene of further dialogue, request and response between God and man. There is no end to love. It is an eternal river.

When we understand prayer in this way and learn to pray in this way, then the problem of whether prayer is heard no longer

[1] Matt. v. 2–11.

exists at all. For what should be meant by the invocation 'Our Father' being heard? Would that be a second thing supplementary to what happens when in faith we say 'Abba, Father'? Is not this itself the fulfilling and hearing of all prayers: even the presence of the Holy Spirit, the nearness of God? Yet all this is so easily said. As long as we live we have to work unceasingly at the one lesson: that of learning to say wholeheartedly 'Abba, Father'.[1]

Every act of prayer culminates in the offering of the self to God to be used, if this may be, in the accomplishment of God's purpose in the world. This is how the Eucharist ends, in a re-commitment of the believer to God and a fresh alignment of his will with what God is doing in the world. And of course this is no *end*, it is a beginning of new work for God. Prayer passes into active love; that is its 'end', in the complex sense of answer, meaning, purpose, fulfilment. The meanings of the Eucharist are carried by a food-symbolism, whose power reaches back into the depths of time and the unconscious, in the light of which prayer can be seen as meant to sustain, as something in the strength of which one goes some distance in this world-wilderness.

There is a fine ambiguity in the ending of the Roman rite. The words '*Ite, missa est*' contain two meanings—'go, the mass is over' and 'go, you are sent out into the world again', and this implies that something has happened to us to make our going into the world in this new access of grace a matter of hope for the world. Certainly we go from the Eucharist pledged to serve Christ in the world and resolved afresh to do his will, so often so cruelly clear, sometimes known only with huge difficulty. Prayer is desire submitted to God along with the desiring self, and it culminates in the desirer's intention to be divested of egotism and completely identified with God and his purpose. Thereafter the prayer will pass into such action as the believer's situation demands or his recent regaining of the spiritual bearings of his life suggests.

Sometimes it is not clear that anything is to be done that is closely associated with the subject of our prayer. When a believer has prayed about, say, the mental or moral disintegration of a friend, or the ending of a war in some part of the world, or the unity of the Church, or about someone desperately ill far

[1] Gerhard Ebeling, *The Lord's Prayer in Today's World*, pp. 56-7.

away, there is often nothing to be done immediately that can be seen as in any way closely related to these matters. But the love and concern which motivated the prayer can act in areas of need close at hand and, in making some clearing or joy in that particular segment of life, he can believe that the whole of life (which includes these distant concerns he cannot directly serve) is that much nearer God's will and sensitive to his creative spirit. A westerner's prayer for peace in the Far East may well be answered by God's asking some service from him there and then which, again, he must try to do 'in his name'. Every prayer has in this way some kind of response from God which in turn, if heeded, makes a new situation of potential prayer and response again and again to the last shorter day of our earthly lives.

This idea of prayer as moving into immediate co-operation with God has been very satisfactorily expounded in the work of Jean Pierre de Caussade called *Abandonment to Divine Providence*.[1] De Caussade was a Jesuit who lived and worked in or near Toulouse from 1675 to 1751, and he is known principally for this remarkable book. The first part of the book consists of his teaching; the second part is a series of letters of spiritual direction addressed to nuns of The Visitation at Nancy. He had been stationed at Nancy, and when he was called away he continued by letters a sensitive and penetrating ministry to these nuns who were striving so hard for Christian perfection and were so disturbed about their failures.

The letters were treasured with great care and published about a century after his death. An English translation first appeared in 1921.

De Caussade's conviction is that true sanctity consists in our total abandonment to divine providence in whatever shape it comes to us moment by moment, that is to say, in a complete Christian adaptation to reality.

This abandonment has two aspects. The first is acceptance. This means reminding ourselves that whatever our present situation is, it is, in fact, God's will for us, and therefore the best that could happen in the circumstances. 'For those things that happen at each moment by the divine command or permission are always the most holy, the best and the most divine for us.'[2]

---

[1] Catholic Records Press, Exeter, 3rd English edition.
[2] Op. cit., p. 6.

Accordingly, we are to surrender ourselves to each wave of the sea of life as it comes with its crest of foam and heart of blue towards us, and with complete confidence. It is Love's word to us all the time, even when we hate it.

The second aspect is co-operation with God. This means finding out what God wants us to do in the present situation and doing it in faith. De Caussade makes much of the fact that for most of us, most of the time, doing God's will is nothing more startling than fidelity to the ordinary claims and duties of every ordinary day. He wryly observes that people often overlook the daily duties of their state in life as being irrelevant to sanctity.[1]

From this follows what is the characteristic theme in de Caussade's teaching, that the way to holiness, and to happiness (for Christians they are the same thing) is to concentrate on the present moment.

The present moment is the only moment in which any kind of action is possible. If I want to do the will of God I must recognize that the divine will is always something I must do *now*. I cannot receive now what God offered me yesterday; I cannot receive now what God will offer me tomorrow. But I can receive now what he is offering me now. And each moment God is offering me some grace for my acceptance or some command for my obedience. Sanctity is simply a matter of receiving the grace and obeying the command presented to us moment by moment. For this important conviction de Caussade coined the phrase 'the sacrament of the present moment'.[2] Like a sacrament, the present moment is the veil of God and conceals the Real Presence, though the reverse way of putting it is equally valid—that the present moment is the unveiling of God and reveals the Real Presence. We may say, 'O that I knew where I might find him!' But in the very moment in which I make this classic *cri de coeur* God is presenting himself to me under the cover of some pain to be endured or some pleasure to be enjoyed or some duty to be fulfilled to his glory. It is in our sufferings, of course, that God is concealed or disguised most thoroughly, but, for that very reason (because we shall tend to assume his absence) he is to be regarded as particularly real and active there, offering us special helps and inspirations appropriate to

[1] Op. cit., pp. 13–14.
[2] Op. cit., pp. 3, 15, 27–9, 57 and *passim*.

our need with an uncanny relevance. And he who trusts and accepts the offered grace will learn that behind the weird mask of pain is the face of Love.

So what is recommended is a continual active and passive co-operation with God moment by moment. We are to attend to each experience as it comes and to God's will in it, and to nothing else. When the swift flow of the river of time takes it from under our gaze we are to let it go and leave it and our action in it to God's mercy while we give ourselves to the next situation that comes to us, with its grace, with its pain (perhaps) and its command. The person who lives this way, as 'simple and straightforward souls' have always done, will gradually find that everything is co-operating to draw him to God.

The acceptance which de Caussade recommends would be completely misunderstood as a stoical resignation to whatever happens. It is a much more active affair than that. It is a matter of consciously approving and actively *willing* what happens to us *because* it comes as God's will for us here and now, and because God is believed to be speaking in it. 'Things, in fact, proceed from the mouth of God like words.'[1]

God's will for us in some painful situation may, of course, be to take steps to get out of it, or change it; and if we are responsive to him we shall know that that is his word to us in that hour. But the unpleasant situation has to be accepted first, and accepted until we feel that it is God's will that we do something about altering it. When that insight comes, we have then to accept the whole situation of being in a difficulty that has to be mastered or removed, and the necessary output of energy for this.

Everyone knows that if you are in a difficulty and you actively will this adverse turn of events, are willing for it to be the case, and begin dealing with it in that mood, you are much more likely to solve it or master it than if you tackle it in a mood of angry hostility to the whole situation. To reject experience is one of the most common ways of rejecting God.

The person who thrusts life away from him, or tries to do so (because it refuses to be disowned), acquires the unmistakeable bitterness of those who resent the way things are with them. This is the well-trodden path to hell, it leads out of grace and into an appalling blindness.

[1] Op. cit., p. 29.

De Caussade's view of prayer is correspondingly simple and direct. God himself and his will are the only things that matter in prayer, as in life. The centre of prayer is accordingly the simple want of God, the desire for the closest possible adherence to his will, and the readiness to obey his signified will moment by moment. Anyone who prays in this way must necessarily find prayer and life continually flowing into each other. Not that many of us manage to live as we pray. But this is the Christian idea. It is up to the critics to find a better one.

Christian perfection cannot be anything else than that we should do God's will and that he should work his will in us. If that happens it is difficult to see what more anyone can possibly want. If it does not happen, it is nevertheless in the Christian view the only thing really worth wanting, though in the playground of desire we mess about with many substitutes. In the occasional moments of understanding that come to us we suspect that there cannot be anything better than having God.

As we have seen, this is one kind of prayer that cannot fail to be granted, so that we are at that point at which the problem of unanswered prayer cannot arise. If it is God we are asking for, we get what we want. It is believed that God comes the moment he is asked for. The specific form in which God gives himself is of course infinitely varied, often disconcerting, sometimes desolating. But to have faith means to believe that all through his nature and his name is love. 'The life of faith is nothing less than the continued pursuit of God through all that disguises, disfigures and, so to say, annihilates him.'[1]

To this theme de Caussade continually returns, to the necessity of perpetually renewing one's confidence in God and one's endeavour to see in each experience some manifestation of his will. The influence of his approach to the spiritual life continues to spread. In *The Spiritual Letters of Dom John Chapman* there is much helpful exposition of de Caussade's teaching, though the book is to be commended apart from this. Chapman, who was Abbot of Downside, came across *Abandonment to Divine Providence* quite late in life and thereafter was continually expounding it in the remarkable ministry of instruction in prayer which he exercised. The idea of the sacrament of the present moment plays an important part in C. S. Lewis's writing about religion. He found

[1] J. P. de Caussade, *Abandonment to Divine Providence*, p. 18.

it in the books of George Macdonald, and it figures repeatedly in the book of selections from Macdonald's writings which Lewis edited. Readers of the work of Evelyn Underhill, Olive Wyon and Dom Christopher Butler will recognize their indebtedness to de Caussade. The same stream of truth can be found in Von Hügel's *Letters to a Niece*, and in the eight groups of profitable reflections at the end of Wesley's *A Plain Account of Christian Perfection*. Indeed, this vein of thought which rejects the conventional concept of 'answers to prayer' is to be found so frequently in Christian writing that it is a cause of amazement that it has not influenced general Christian attitude more.

> The immediate person thinks and imagines that when he prays, the important thing, the thing he must concentrate upon, is that *God should hear what he is praying for*. And yet in the true, eternal sense it is just the reverse: the true relation in prayer is achieved not when God hears what is prayed for, but when *the person praying* continues to pray until he is *the one who hears*, who hears what God wills. The immediate person, therefore, uses many words and therefore makes demands in his prayer; the true man of prayer only *attends*.[1]

And there is an earlier voice that speaks in the same tone:

> You, who are truth, reside everywhere to answer all who ask counsel of you, and in one act reply to all, though all seek counsel on different matters. And you answer clearly, but all do not hear clearly. All ask what they wish, but do not always hear the answer that they wish. That man is your best servant who is not so much concerned to hear from you what he wills as to will what he hears from you.[2]

Throughout the tradition of Christian spirituality there are many claims that the rewards are greater than our dreams. And this expectation is found in scripture, it is expressed in more than one collect in the liturgy, and it forms part of the continual surprise of Christian believers:

> God usually answers our prayers so (much more) according to the measure of his own magnificence than of our asking, that we do not know his boons to be those for which we besought him.[3]

[1] *The Journals of Kierkegaard, 1834–1854* (Fontana Books), p. 97.
[2] *The Confessions of St. Augustine* (trans. F. J. Sheed), p. 188.
[3] Coventry Patmore, *The Rod, the Root, and the Flower*, p. 230.

There is much to be gained from realizing life's notable ability to deceive us. We often pray and think we have not been 'answered'. Believers should have confidence in God and appeal to him even when this does not seem to make sense. If they persevere they will find that the 'answers' come, though possibly in a very different form from the one they expected.[1]

St. Augustine was deeply aware of this psychological and theological fact—the psychological aspect being that there is far more in any of our desires than the point of yearning and demand that presses into consciousness, the theological aspect being that God understands this better than we and often 'answers' the deeper desire that for some reason has not penetrated into what we know of ourselves but is in fact more truly 'us' than the want whose imperious burning currently throws the mind into a conflict of painful yes and no. When Augustine wanted to go to Rome, Monica tried to prevent him leaving, but he (not without much emotional pain) eluded her and left her actually praying that he would not leave her. 'But', St. Augustine continues in his *Confessions*,[2] 'you saw deeper and granted the essential of her prayer: you did not do what she was at the moment asking, that you might do the thing she was always asking.'

There is so much evidence to the believer that in all things God works for his good, that again and again he finds that he has been granted more than he asked or thought. And yet there is a peculiar joy of recognition as the Christian mind reflects on the way things have gone: 'Yes, that is what I really wanted, even when I thought I wanted something quite different.'

---

[1] Romano Guardini, *L'Initiation à la Prière*, p. 90.
[2] *Confessions*, Book v. 8 (trans. F. J. Sheed). Cf. J. Guitton, *The Modernity of St. Augustine*, p. 18.

11

Helps

THERE is nothing like religion for exposing the sometimes inconvenient fact that we are individuals. People may look all the same coming *en masse* from a football match, but as soon as any one of that crowd begins honestly to think about God he functions with all the preference and idiosyncrasy that make every human being unique.

Christian taste in literature that is used to build up faith is as sharp and definite as the reaction to sugar or perfume. As soon as things begin to matter deeply, people's differences emerge. And nowhere is this more obvious than in the most personal dimensions of religious experience, prayer and the Eucharist. Consequently the least useful part of books about prayer is always that which attempts to suggest practical helps. What helps one person revolts the next. What is useful to us at one stage of our life may bore or infuriate us later.

There has always been a tradition of spiritual reading in the Methodist Church. John Wesley began his Christian Library (ninety books) for this purpose, and an admirable selection it was. In Victorian and Edwardian England in devout Methodist homes you would find Wesley's sermons, the lives of Wesley's preachers, the Hymn Book, Thomas à Kempis's *Imitation*, William Law's *Serious Call*, Bunyan's *Pilgrim's Progress*, Henry Drummond's *The Greatest Thing in the World*, and books of sermons—usually much more solid doctrinally and more elegant stylistically than books of sermons published today. In the poorest homes, religious weeklies, like the *Sunday Companion*, had an important place in believers' attempts to nourish their faith. Certain established authors were thought to be spiritually elevating—George Eliot, Dickens, Mark Rutherford. And much of this has simply gone out of fashion.

The equivalent today is the paperback religious book. Works by C. S. Lewis, Bonhoeffer, Barclay, in paperback may be just as much read when allowance has been made for the smaller believing community. The names that appear in the bibliographies of the classical spiritual writers, St. Ignatius, St. Francis de Sales, Scupoli, Fénelon, do not seem to help either laity or clergy very much now. But the paperback revolution in publishing has made available more books suitable for 'spiritual reading' than ever before. Because this kind of reading is so important in building up and maintaining a Christian attitude to life, Christian believers simply have to rummage through it, trying this and that, until they find something to their taste. The one point that can be made with certainty is that they will eventually find that only a very few books will survive in their interest as books to which they return frequently. It appears that Brother Lawrence's *Practice of the Presence of God* and Thomas à Kempis's *Imitation of Christ* continue to be used generation after generation. I remember a very sophisticated non-church-going woman telling me that she always kept Thomas à Kempis's *Imitation* on her bedside table and read a few lines of it most nights 'as a reminder of all I could never be'.

I myself have returned most frequently to St. Augustine's *Confessions*, de Caussade's *Abandonment to Divine Providence*, certain poems of Herbert and Vaughan, and John Donne's *Devotions* (though with the latter I cannot disentangle the marvel of the author's use of our beautiful English language from the 'spirituality' which is when considered by itself somewhat melancholy).

The Bible is an extremely difficult book for use in private prayer. As biblical scholarship advances the Bible becomes increasingly fascinating to *study*, but so much work is involved in this study that the only profitable way in which Christians can now attempt it is through group study in the weekday life of the Church or individually with a commentary that is not too academic. We certainly need more commentaries like William Temple's *Readings in St. John's Gospel*.

Much of the Bible is second-rate literature which we would not dream of reading if it were, for example, part of the literature of classical Greece and Rome, unless we were students within a tradition which required the reading of *all* the extant literature of a period (as students of the Classics at universities still have to read such second-rate authors as Menander, Plautus and Ennius).

The book of Genesis, the Joseph and David sagas, the Psalms, the book of Job, and some of the visions of Isaiah, Jeremiah and Ezekiel, are enough for the average believer who is reading the Old Testament in the attempt to increase his knowledge of God and to advance in the life of love. The rest is, of course, full of substance for people who read it with antiquarian interests or like studying the history of the Christian religion, but that is quite another matter. Christian believers who are using the New Testament for private spiritual reading are well advised to concentrate on the four lives of Jesus. This is not to say that they should not attempt more but there is not much to be gained from attempting the epistles otherwise than in serious study within some organized church study-group.

All of this means that we need a new kind of lectionary for private devotion that is not based on the principle that certain words should be read because they are in the Bible but that they should be read because they are found to feed the Christian mind.

There is a vast field of literature that helps to build up a Christian imagination in the general category of 'good literature' —not 'good' in the sense of 'improving' or 'useful as a present for some fading aunt' but in the sense of using words well, attending seriously to the distinction between good and evil, compassionate about our human predicament (after all, who is there to turn to when the worst happens?), aware of the incongruities and reversals and satisfactions that make human beings laugh, deeply conscious of the impenetrable mystery in which human life is lived, and liable to leave that disturbance in the mind out of which thoughts about the meaning of existence naturally arise.[1] A Christian of today who can benefit from reading Albert Camus's *The Plague* will find it far more important to his life of faith than reading the minor prophets. How true the word 'minor' is there! And Camus was neither a Jew nor a Christian. The forsaking of the Church for the realm of the arts is one of the characteristic works of the Holy Spirit in our generation.

Where do we look now for faithful, stimulating, profound accounts of what it is to be alive in the twentieth century? The inevitable answer to that question carries a judgement. We look to

[1] Cf. Reginald Cant, *The Churchman's Companion*, pp. 224–5.

the poet or novelist or dramatist or film producer. In creative works of art we see ourselves anew, come to understand ourselves better and come into touch with just those sources of imagination which should nourish efforts in natural theology. The best text-books for contemporary natural theologians are not the second-hand theological treatises but the living works of artists who are in touch with the springs of creative imagination. This is only another way of saying that theologians cannot direct men's minds to God until they are themselves steeped in God's world and in the imaginative productions of his most sensitive and articulate creatures.[1]

Reading is not the only means of renewing the mind and disposing it to love life more. There is the enjoyment of music, painting, drama and all the arts. There is the world of recreation. It is at this point that the clichés about praying while gardening or walking in the country have some relevance, though they need to be re-stated. It is not that these activities are themselves forms of prayer or certain to stimulate it, much less that they are substitutes for it, but that they are forms of happiness, some of them forms of the deepest happiness known to man. And deep happiness purifies and renews the mind, stops its silent egotistical monologue, and often leads it into that range of experience in which 'the world loses its ordinariness and takes on a disturbing, derivative, transfigured look; when awe deepens into numinous awe; when our response is incommensurate with what we should judge normally to be before us'.[2] Happiness of this kind is as good a propaideutic as any for wanting to love God or wanting to love him more.

People in whom, through the chance influences of their education and upbringing, God has awakened the enjoyment of music, painting, poetry, drama, should use these tastes deliberately in their fostering of their religious life. They are people to whom much has been given and from whom we are told much will be required and obviously is now required. Their enjoyment of these areas of experience is rightly seen as their willing and happy contemplation of God in one or other of his innumerable aspects. The Holy Spirit articulates far more successfully through Bach and Beethoven than through the bore-

[1] H. E. Root, *Soundings* (ed. Vidler), p. 18.
[2] Ronald Hepburn, 'The Gospel and the Claims of Logic', *The Listener*, 11th April 1963.

dom of the books of Chronicles. But those who have been given so much, who can so happily contemplate the beauty of the natural world and the infinite fascination of human artefacts should realize that this is simply evidence of God's unfathomable mercy to them in investing their lives with influences to develop this marvellously satisfying response to the beautiful. There must surely follow from this a due humility and thankfulness, and the drive to work so that more people may have the same good fortune, the same diversity of joy in their lives.

Books of prayers are an essential help to the life of private prayer. Some people are reluctant to use them because they have been told that this is less sincere than praying in one's own words. As a general guide for prayer it would be very difficult to establish the superiority of one's own words over those in the great treasury of Christian prayer. It is true that there will be times when saying other people's words for our prayers may not be as good for us as saying our own, but most of the time it is in fact better, because generally they are much better words and better suited to the purpose for which they are being used.

The idea of words as a form of private property is peculiar. The words 'I love you' do not belong to anybody. All over the world hundreds of people are using them at this moment, using a familiar phrase from love's ceremony because it says what they want to say. It is not theirs, or ours when we use it, but all of us use it, just as in another situation we may want to use the words 'according to thy loving kindness blot out my transgressions'.

Such phrases and sentences become 'our own' in the degree to which we put ourselves into the saying. Sincerity has nothing whatever to do with authorship, spontaneity or originality. It has to do with the amount of oneself one is able to put into a word, a look, an action.

One of the chronic and humiliating difficulties in praying springs from the fact that we have so little control over our minds. Very few people can give their religious thought and aspiration a verbal form in the mind for any length of time even when faith and love are strong in them. When the flow of such thought dries up, since the mind cannot be empty, other material automatically flows in. It is often said that this other material will generally be related to areas of our personal life which in fact need to be offered to God again and again and that therefore it can forthwith be made the subject of prayer. This suggestion is not as bright as it seems, because it presupposes a control over the movement of the mind that has in fact been lost.

The use of books of prayer is not only helpful, but for most people essential. The memorizing of prayers is an even greater help—favourite prayers, and prayers that express various religious moods and attitudes in a form that is congenial to us. Words are then to hand when one sets oneself to pray, there is a track for the mind in its uncertainty to travel along, and the struggle is reduced to the single task of putting as much of oneself as one can into the fine and familiar words. It is much to be regretted that the practice of learning by heart (prayers, Bible passages, poetry, even points from the catechism)[1] does not commend itself to our generation. All who adopt it know it to be a spiritual investment that proves its worth continually.

There are so many books of prayers and they vary so much that it is very difficult to recommend particular ones. Once again this factor of variation in spiritual taste operates strongly, and there is no more to say to people who want help than that they must look at some of this vast literature and see if there is anything at all that appeals to them. The books themselves are invariably unequal in quality; they may contain one or two prayers which one immediately and gladly makes 'one's own' but the rest may be quite nauseating. Just now, for example, a number of people seem to find Michel Quoist's *Prayers of Life* (a set of meditations and aspirations relating to contemporary situations) useful, others find this kind of thing naïve and sentimental and characteristic of a certain strain of French spirituality, in the tradition of Charles Péguy's *Prières*, which is too verbose. It is impossible to discuss this subject without revealing personal bias.

The most useful prayers for directing the mind to God or associating present experience with one's convictions about God are prayers which are brief, say succinctly that which they are composed to say, and say it with dignity and some bloom of relevant emotion—but not so beautifully that one is distracted

---

[1] E.g. The Methodist Senior Catechism, question no. 55, if memorized and pondered, would be of incalculable service to many people.

from the meaning by the artistry of the style. Traditional Free Church public prayer (and its derivative in the prayer meeting) is on the whole tediously verbose, exhortatory, and far more like preaching than praying. The weakness of much Roman Catholic prayer is the paucity of its content. But the great prayers of Christendom somehow survive. People find themselves able and willing to say them at any age and in every century. There are not many of these, but this does not seem to matter. Indeed, prayer is a form of human expression in which progress does not seem to be made in the normal way at all; occasionally someone in some century finds words to express a certain religious attitude and it just happens that people can go on using those words for generations. For the rest, Christian prayer is occasional, ephemeral, serving its purpose perhaps adequately in the moment but not invested with any continuing life in the mind of the Church.

> Not one good prayer has been composed, either by Catholic or by Protestant, since the days of the Reformation. The additions to the Breviary, since the Council of Trent, have no ray of divine insight; and the manuals of devotion compiled since then, by authority or otherwise, are enough to drive a sensible Christian crazy by their extravagance and unreality.[1]

Once this is understood and accepted, the believer must simply look around for prayers that seem to express what he wants to say to God. Some of the classical prayers will do this for him. But, in his need of the stimulus of variety, he will be lucky if he finds a volume that satisfies him. The Pelican book of prayers[2] is as good as any. But there is much to be said for making one's own, collecting in some notebook the prayers that say what one wants to say to God most frequently. It is a valuable spiritual exercise to write one's thoughts, wishes and complaints about God. Certainly it is an illumination and encouragement periodically to make a list of those experiences in our lives in which, on reflection, we conclude that we might well then have been with God, some of them so beautiful that they were infinitely exhilarating and humiliating at the same time, some of them quite horrible.

[1] Coventry Patmore, *The Rod, the Root and the Flower*, p. 50.
[2] *Daily Prayer* (ed. Milner-White and Briggs).

It may seem a small point, but the spiritual life is in constant need of freshness and, in this need, if one has another language at one's command, it is a help to know and use prayers in another language. Certainly it is a help to pray in ways that are not part of one's familiar religious tradition, which of course involves finding out how other Christians have prayed and, with interest and love, learning from them.

One of the admirable results of the ecumenical movement and the opportunity Christians are now given to explore the good things in other traditions than the one in which they have been brought up is that they are now free to try some of the helps to faith other Christians have found useful. And it is in fact now happening that helps to prayer and forms of devotional life of which Methodists have grown tired (simply because the religious mind needs varied fare to keep alive) are now interesting other Churches and being adopted by them. Similarly, Methodists might profitably use some of the helps other Churches have perhaps similarly over-used and consequently found increasingly ineffective.

Some time ago an article in the Roman Catholic Newsletter *Search*[1] discussed the boredom which many Romans find with their traditional pieties, such as the Rosary ('merely a monotonous and boring relic of past ages when few could read'), and ended by making recommendations which looked horrifyingly familiar to a Methodist, such as more extempore prayer, weekday preaching services, some kind of class-meeting—the very things that have died on us.

All this is promising. Part of the price we have paid for disunity is that we have been (in a sense) forbidden to nourish our spiritual life on any other fare than that produced by our own co-operative society, and we have simply grown tired of it. Unity must mean a sharing of each other's knowledge, and the fun of savouring some strange tastes whose very strangeness can bring a new interest into our devotional life and even the possibility of finding helps to prayer for which we may have been vainly looking for years.

In this much to be desired exchange of valuables, Methodists might consider taking the Rosary into their system. And certainly some are already doing this. It is an interesting question

[1] *Search*, March 1965, pp. 404–10.

how they could ever have begun such a (to them) outlandish lark.

Not many of them know that John Wesley himself used the Rosary; and the one he used is at present to be found among the archives of The Leys School, Cambridge. But a much more important 'carrier' of this new form of prayer has been a book by an Anglican theologian, Austin Farrer, titled *Lord, I believe.* This book is a series of suggestions for turning the Creed into prayer. It is a helpful book, to be recommended optimistically for spiritual reading. But its last two chapters concern the Rosary, how Anglicans might use it, and suggest extensions and additions to its traditional use. Incidentally, the author shows how it is usable by people to whom the direct invocation of the mother of our Lord is an uncongenial form of prayer. These chapters have certainly interested many protestants beyond the Anglican communion and stimulated them to begin using the Rosary.

Another influence has been the growth of interest in an Eastern Orthodox practice, somewhat similar to the western Rosary, known as the 'Jesus prayer'. This consists in the repetition of the sentence 'Lord Jesus Christ, son of God, have mercy on me, a sinner', though the prayer is usually said without the last two words, is often reduced to the simple invocation of the name of Jesus, and can be used with beads or without them. This practice has received an unexpected popularization, interesting but not particularly profound, in J. D. Salinger's best-selling novel *Franny and Zooey*. Uninstructed use of the 'Jesus prayer' could result in its becoming an obsessional formula with pathological potentiality. But when it is used by a person whose mind is soaked in the Bible, for whom the many scriptural connotations of the words 'Lord', 'Jesus' and of the idea of 'name' are the subject of frequent thought outside prayer, it can easily be imagined what a means of grace this prayer must be. A monk of the Eastern Church has written a pamphlet that admirably shows this and is in itself a fine example of 'spiritual reading'.[1]

The western Rosary is a form of prayer that can be used

[1] *On the Invocation of the Name of Jesus*, (publ. The Fellowship of St. Alban & St. Sergius); Cf. V. Lossky, *The Mystical Theology of the Eastern Church*, pp. 209–11; and Archbishop Anthony Bloom, *Living Prayer*, ch. 6.

almost anywhere, it is simple and easily learned, and its effectiveness as an aid derives from the fact that the hands are given some action, 'the front of the mind' some words to repeat, and the deeper self one or other of the great facts in the Jesus-event to contemplate.

The reading in course even of the New Testament must fail our generation again and again. We cannot now hear the parable of the wise and foolish virgins without a yawn of ineffable boredom. Even the parable of the prodigal son has had most of the life squeezed out of it by preaching and exposition, and one tries to avoid it now—it has such an awful pleading look as it lies on Luke's page wanting to be liked more. But the images in which the great gospel-events are summarized, the annunciation, the birth, the losing of the adolescent boy, the baptism, the offered pact with the devil, the anointing by a woman 'outsider', the prayer from fear to faith in Gethsemane, the arrest, the torture and the foolery, the death, resurrection and revitalizing of the believing community—these events (and others which will spring to any Christian's mind) many of which are so profoundly called 'the mysteries' in Rosary terminology, have assumed an inexhaustible concentration of meaning in the Christian religion.

They are the basic Christian images which have been found to mediate the presence and word of God for all the Christian generations. They suggest more than they denote. They are like sacraments, not mere signs or symbols, but efficacious signs, they participate in the power and communicate the presence they describe. They have a mysterious relatedness to innumerable facts in deepest human experience as well as an apparently unlimited scope as articulations of Christian understanding of God. They hint at meanings which do not seem to be made present to the mind in other ways. For example, there is a fantastic concentration of meaning in the word 'annunciation' to a Christian whose imagination connects it first with 'The Annunciation' but is open to the multiplicity of extra-scriptural significances this joyful and dreadful word has.

At the same time these images do not require always to be meditated at length. Indeed their spiritual power is greater when they are simply contemplated than when they are discursively expounded. And yet it is frequently found that when the Rosary is said with some special intention, by someone concerned about his family or his friend or some personal crisis of his own, the prescribed 'mysteries' of the day provide thoughts in which faith hears the word of God for the issue that is currently burning the mind.

It is a notable feature of Christian prayer that it should be so much a continually renewed attention to certain images and groups of words intrinsically of the greatest importance in Christian faith and, because of this, made even more potent by the fact that they have carried the emotional storms and calms of millions of lives struggling after the perfection of Christ. The result is that a Christian does not need many prayers so much as to know and use a few more and more deeply. The great moments of the Liturgy, the confession, the sursum corda, the sanctus, the creed, the gloria, the 'Our Father', with that small collection of prayers we have gathered because they seem to express our mind when we wish to turn to God—these are enough for most of us. The odd thing is that one has to buy a terrible lot of books of prayers to come to this realization.

Of all these the 'Our Father' is the one we need to use over and over again, working our way into its depths of meaning, putting up with the times when it means nothing at all but a familiar jingle, reading any devout, scholarly, imaginative comment on it we can find, and never losing the faith that it holds all that anybody needs to know. All of Christianity is there explicitly or implicitly. A voice speaks in it that is beyond this world, yet intimately associated with all this world's pain and pleasure, and when we say it we are attempting a marvellous thing, which is to address God with the words of the son of God, trying to adopt that posture before reality for which God gave us life in this world. And it continues, every so often, to flood certain people with an amazement that amounts to a revelation, so that it becomes a kind of converting ordinance. This is from Edwin Muir's autobiography:

> Last night, going to bed alone, I suddenly found myself . . . reciting the Lord's Prayer in a loud, emphatic voice—a thing I had not done for many years—with deep urgency and profound disturbed emotion. While I went on I grew more composed; as if it had been empty and craving and were being replenished, my soul grew still; every word had a strange fullness of meaning which

astonished and delighted me . . . meaning after meaning sprang from it, overcoming me again with joyful surprise; and I realized that this simple petition was always universal and always inexhaustible, and day by day sanctified human life.[1]

And these are the conclusions of Simone Weil:

The Our Father contains all possible petitions; we cannot conceive of any prayer which is not already contained in it. It is to prayer what Christ is to humanity. It is impossible to say it once through, giving the fullest possible attention to each word, without a change, infinitesimal perhaps but real, taking place in the soul.[2]

We have already seen how private prayer is a derivative of corporate prayer and that much of the liturgy has traditionally entered into a Christian's thoughts as he attempts to see his personal situation in the light of Christian thankfulness and offering. The use of the great acts of the liturgy has been consistently recommended for the life of private prayer. It has always been the basis of private prayer in Orthodoxy. And it is by this means that Orthodoxy has traditionally bound into 'togetherness' (a term of special ificance in Eastern Christendom) liturgy and private devn, and monastic communities and those living 'in the world'.[3]

There is a vast literature concerning the various ways in which Christians in the west have prayed. A very useful compendium of these, though it is far more valuable than a mere compendium, is *The Art of Mental Prayer* by Bede Frost.[4] There is no better introduction to the classical western tradition of prayer and meditation. It is difficult to say how much, if any, of this is helpful or even possible for Christians today. Certainly meditation, in the traditional western modes, originating as they do from the monastic world, seems a decreasing possibility for our generation. This tradition of meditation has never existed in the Orthodox Church, though there is a vigorous tradition of morning and evening prayer before the ikon in Orthodox homes.[5] The formal schematization of meditation be-

[1] Edwin Muir, *An Autobiography*, p. 246.
[2] Simone Weil, *Waiting on God* (Routledge, 1951), p. 153.
[3] T. Ware, *The Orthodox Church*, p. 310.
[4] Publ. S.P.C.K.
[5] T. Ware, *The Orthodox Church*, pp. 310, 312.

longs to western Christendom, and probably to its past, except in the life of the religious orders.

Methodists have traditionally done their equivalent of meditation together. In this form it has had a very important place in Methodist spirituality, by means of the sermon in Sunday worship, the address in the weekday fellowship, and in the dialogue of the class-meeting. It is interesting that the traditional (now largely abandoned) form of the sermon had a shape so closely related to the classical methods of meditation (i.e. prelude, three points, and application) that one is inclined to assume that in some subterranean way it was influenced by them.

But these forms of meditation have a decreasing power among us. Their place is being taken by (1) the private reading of the Bible with leaflets of brief notes issued by organizations like the International Bible Reading Association and the Bible Reading Fellowship, though one suspects that this kind of help is much less effective than it used to be, mainly because the people who write the notes are so patronizing and 'talk down' too much to their audience; (2) and much more satisfactorily, the study of the Bible in Church study-group under trained leadership; or (3) the study of the Bible in a class-meeting without trained leadership. It is astonishing how profitable is the practice of a group of eight or ten people reading together a short passage of the gospel and then leaving time for thinking about it without the help of commentaries, and then expressing the questions, convictions, resentments which the words they have read have excited in their minds.

Certainly the most widely used help today is the reading of paperback devotional literature and Christian apologetic. It is not meditation in the old sense. But it is proving a great source of help and interest to Christians and inquirers of our time and must be one of the principal channels of the word of God in this generation. Of course, this reading need not be done daily, but it is wise for the believer to have some such book of spiritual reading on the go all the time along with his other reading.

Some offering of the coming day to God in the morning, in confidence and in welcome of life, is a Christian thing to do. It need not take long. Some offering of the remembered day to God in the evening seems right (What has today amounted to?

121

Have I really cared about anything? Have I had joy? What agitates me about it?), and then some act of gratitude, confession and re-commitment. This again need not take long. Suitable words are to be found in the books of prayers, or we can make our own if we prefer. It is best to use memorized prayer so that books are not necessary at these points of the day. It should be remembered that the sign of the cross is one of the briefest and most concentrated summaries of Christian memory, affection and commitment.

It is possible to develop the habit of naturally, throughout each day, associating particular moments of experience and people met or remembered with the thought of God and his will. And this form of momentary praying, without much verbal formulation, is the commonest form of praying for most people in our time. There is some discussion of this in the pamphlet, to which we have already referred, *Prayer for busy people*.[1]

One of the most acute needs of Christian believers today is that the liturgical experts should provide them with a brief morning and evening office that can be easily learned and expresses what a Christian may rightly say to God and may conceivably want to say.[2] No doubt an act of committal to God before sleep and an act of welcome of life on waking are right uses of prayer, but they are objectionable when expressed in the request that God will 'keep us safe' during the night and in morning thanksgiving that by God's shattering providence one has been allowed to resume consciousness.

If people worship regularly with the Church, use its teaching ministry, maintain some reading that is directed towards building themselves up in the faith, and especially if they make use of such helps as sacramental confession and an annual retreat, they do not need to spend long in private prayer unless they feel some special *attrait* in this direction.

Ministers are in a very different position, compared with most of their people, in that they have such advantages as a study, privacy and books at hand. It is part of their ministry that they should pray in addition to its being part of their discipleship as Christians. Many people ask for their prayers and rely on being

[1] John Townroe, a reprint from *Theology*, publ. S.P.C.K.
[2] This is being undertaken by the Joint Liturgical Group consisting of representatives of the main British confessions with a Roman Catholic observer.

remembered and loved in this characteristically Christian way. And it must not be possible to endure the terrible responsibility into which ordination plunges them without prayer. Of course, there must be some and may be many who struggle on without this help, for temperamental reasons or because they have not found any congenial method; but unless this lack is balanced by the gift of some particularly sensitive response to other Christian channels of the presence of God, the Christian mind in them must be easily weakened and at times destroyed.

They have exactly the same difficulty as the layman in that there is no rule that what helps one will help another, they are involved in the same long search for congenial helps to prayer. To recommend is simply to indicate personal preference. It is, however, a common experience that as one grows older the books of prayers one depends on become fewer and are drawn from the basic tradition. Certainly the bright contemporary prayers that create a stir for a while die quickest, while the *Book of Common Prayer*, a compendium like the *Priest's Book of Private Devotion*, Lancelot Andrewes's *Preces Privatae*, *The Missal*, an anthology like *Daily Prayer* (Pelican Books) persist in being wanted. There will always be people who want very different fare, more contemporary, less covered with Christian dust. But they have a weary, even dreary search on hand.

It is a relief to remember that no books are required for the simplest form of prayer, which is contemplation. It consists simply in placing the self in the presence of God by an act of faith and then 'deliberately giving attention to attributes or conditions of God's being. Words, titles, adjectives describing them, or mysteries, may be used. But these are not very important; they are means of keeping in the presence. Part of the time passes without formulated thought; and intense concentration is self-defeating'.[1] The prevailing tone is appreciation, praise, contentment, renewal of trust. At first it is possible to do this for only a very short time, but with use of this method of being still and 'knowing' that God is God the time so spent automatically extends. It is suitably ended with some act of praise like 'Glory be to the Father . . .'. It is usually helpful to be in a holy place.

[1] Fr. Henry Cooper, Master of the Royal Foundation of St. Katharine, in some as yet unpublished seminar notes.

It is currently fashionable to suspect the idea of a 'holy' place, because it suggests a division between the sacred and the secular. There are voices to be heard just now that press this attitude so persistently that one would conclude that a church is no more a 'holy' place than a departmental store, a cinema, or a slaughterhouse—which simply shows how screamingly funny up-to-date religion can be.

It has always been part of the Christian use of praying that some understanding of 'the place of prayer' is important. The place of prayer is 'in the Spirit',[1] that is to say 'in the holy spirit', which in turn means that the place of prayer is constituted entirely by the fact that a human being in joy or need turns to God of whom he has (maybe only very remotely) heard through Jesus Christ, whom he cannot see at all but believes to be around within below above him like an atmosphere, but far more definitively endowed with attributes than the word 'atmosphere' suggests. In this context of thought contemporary immanentists are right, and it *is* possible to pray to God in a departmental store, a cinema and (?) a slaughterhouse.

But the fact remains that in Christian experience people wish to be able to pray far more frequently than they actually find themselves wanting to pray, and that therefore any kind of stimulus is to be welcomed. And one stimulus to prayer is to be in a holy place, made holy not just by the fact of formal consecration but because for centuries human beings in the mystery of their multitude and solitude have one after another knelt here in happiness or misery and attempted to relate their condition to what they had been taught about God.

Methodists have no knowledge of this particular help within their own tradition. They have no tradition of using the Church as a place of private prayer, and consequently their churches are devoid of any visual aids to stimulate the religious imagination. But this help can be found in other traditions, churches of other denominations are open during weekdays, and it is possible to use them for a few minutes of 'being in the Presence', in the lunch hour, or before going home from work, or some other time.

This kind of behaviour is sometimes criticized on the ground that it implies a disengagement from 'practical' life. Prayer is no

[1] Cf. R. Guardini, *L'Initiation à la Prière*, p. 31.

more a disengagement from practical life than is the reading of a book, attendance at a symphony concert, or mere relaxation. The idea that 'life' is to be interpreted as that area of experience in which we are doing the daily work for which we are paid or serving the community in some other way than attending to our own needs is the product of a fiendish and myopic puritanism. Much of the popular religious talk about engagement and withdrawal is conducted on a superficial level. 'Engagement' and 'service' can be just as much a withdrawal from life as the dreamiest, most wishfulfilling and escapist kind of prayer. Everyone is 'in life' for better or worse by the mere fact of existing. If a particular *éclat* is to be given to the idea of 'involvement in life' it cannot be constituted by the extent to which paid work and voluntary service dominate each day's hours of consciousness but by one's awareness of the depth and complexity of life, its mystery, problems, beauty, hatefulness, and the attention one gives to these in thought and action. If it can be said of a person going into a city church during his lunch hour to pray that he is 'withdrawing from life', it can equally be said of the person who does not do this but uses all his lunch hour for business consultation with a prospective customer whom he wants to soften up in this way on his firm's expense account, or of the parson who puts on some tatty midday service in his church, that these may well be withdrawing from life. Their behaviour may be the presenting signs of their evasion of important tracts of human experience, while the man in church, being quiet or telling his beads, could be in fact *expanding* his mental universe, exposing himself to a much wider range of experience (not all of it comforting), and therefore being much more mature, realistic and contemporary.

12

Silence, Retreats, Directors, Rules, Time

OUR tradition owes much of its power and its weakness to
the central place assigned in it to the word—the read
word of the Bible, the preached word in the sermon, the
hesitant word that flits across the group in class-meeting as one
and then another bravely attempts to say what he thinks about
God's mysterious being and questionable goings-on. There is
the bright but sometimes tragically shallow word of Christian
greeting and friendship (we can be dying for understanding and
only get words), there is the 'work of God' word in Leaders'
Meeting and Synod that is so often transubstantiated into ver-
biage by some hidden devil in us all, and there is the personal
word, call or pardon the believer waits in the gloom of his
secret need to hear from God.

The dangers in all this might be reduced a little if we had the
tradition of a Religious Order in the life of our communion.
Such a tradition must surely drive people now and again to
think that it is possible to talk oneself out of true living and into
the merest activism. This help God has not given us in Methodism. He has given us a lot of talk.

He has other gifts, of course. But for some years now the
desire for a little silence has been growing among us. Churches
are increasingly finding value in quiet days and even in some
kind of Retreat. When people are persuaded to leave the en-
vironment of their daily life and go some distance into a completely new spiritual situation (especially if it is in beautiful
surroundings and where there is a long tradition of community
prayer) they find that they are able to receive in this isolation
and concentration much more of God than they apparently
receive in the familiar pattern of regular weekly meetings of
worship or instruction in the life of the local church. It is very
likely that this more concentrated and prepared method of
spiritual rehabilitation is going to replace some of the traditional
weekly programmes of the average church.

Such experiments as we have so far made have been generally more like a conference or study-group than a disciplined Retreat. But the desire for silence is being felt, and these experiments increasingly include a period (perhaps a whole day) of silence. This repels or intrigues people according to their spiritual make up and present need, but to those who are intrigued the realization of the value of silence is a moment of true spiritual discovery in their lives. It is the awakening of a thirst that will never leave them, the thirst for silence—'la fontaine qui coule où personne ne passe; mais Dieu y vient boire'.[1]

The discovery of silence is accompanied by the discovery of solitude. Mature human beings need to be alone, and wish to be alone, for some time almost every day. It is a wish for deliberately chosen solitude that is going to be used creatively—not the solitude of the housewife which is entirely constituted by the fact that her husband has gone to work and the children have gone to school so that she just *happens to be alone* in the house, nor that of the person in digs in some city where he has just taken a new job and knows nobody so that he is merely *lonely*. We desire a solitude we choose. And chosen solitude is becoming very difficult to obtain in the twentieth century in which life is lived by so many in small houses or flats, ceaseless noise, a busyness that decreases in satisfaction as it increases in quantity as, no longer in control, they automatically respond to innumerable stimuli. The Retreat is for many believers the only chance they can find in months simply to be alone. It is no wonder that the desire for this experience is growing. Our own people are beginning to make private retreats or join in organized parish retreats in Anglican (and occasionally Roman) Retreat houses. They find that one has to book well in advance.[2]

One of the frequent results of this experience is that in quiet and solitude the true self can hear itself speak (much of the time a phoney self seems to dominate us) and this true self sees what it wants and needs in its life and what it can jettison. There appears the desire to live a more ordered religious life, by some kind of plan or programme, the idea of living by a rule.

For Methodists this is certainly a return to their origins since

[1] Marie Noël, *Notes Intimes*, p. 248.
[2] The Association for Promoting Retreats publishes details of such opportunities in its pamphlet *The Vision* every six months.

one of the most widely known features of the spirit of the early Methodists was their systematic ordering of their personal lives under God. This conscious ordering of life did not begin with John Wesley's (much misunderstood) experience in Aldersgate Street in 1738. Its roots go much deeper, into the disciplined religious life which John Wesley and a few other undergraduates tried to live while up at Oxford, deeper still into the principles by which his mother Susanna ordered the religious life of her family while her husband was either away or writing indifferent poetry, deeper still into the rules of holy living and dying of Jeremy Taylor and all the systematic earnestness of puritan religion, which in turn is vitally connected with that disciplined search for God and Christian perfection which is at the heart of the great religious orders of pre-Reformation Christianity. There are no gaps or breaks in the web of life. The essence of whatever is good in Methodist spirituality is part of this great stream of earnest Christianity which again and again in the history of the Church has expressed itself in the conviction that the only way to be cornered by your promises and to save your dedications from pseudo-religious posturing is by some kind of religious rule.

A rule of life should cover at least six points: some time for daily or weekly prayer, some time for daily or weekly Bible or other spiritual reading, a stipulation that one attends the worship of the Church to which one belongs once a Sunday and particularly its celebrations of the Eucharist, a stipulation about self-examination (for example, cursorily frequently, but with some care during Lent, or quarterly, or monthly, or whatever seems best), the setting aside of a definite proportion of one's income for the service of God in Church and community, personal involvement in some non-Churchy area of social amelioration.

Additional helps in a rule are Friday abstinence from meat, not because anyone can conceivably find any intrinsic merit in this, but because it has been a traditional form of Christian living and so links us with our past and because it helps towards realizing the peculiar aura that Friday carries in the Christian memory. Fasting, though commended by John Wesley, will probably seem to present-day Methodists to have most to commend it when seen as the decision to be reasonable in the indulgence of oneself as a taster and consumer of life (an important aspect of Christian asceticism) and, incidentally, the decision (only relevant normally to people over 40) to keep one's weight at the prescribed medical standard for one's height. Interpreted in this way, fasting, as the avoidance of carbohydrates, is an important part of Christian life in a civilization characterized by an alarming incidence of coronary thrombosis.

A rule should make provision for regular examination 'in Christ' of one's primary human relationships—with one's parents, one's wife or husband, one's children and one's work. These are the areas of life where it is most likely to be disturbed by aggression, resentment, self-deception, ambition; they are in fact principal fields of anxiety.

A rule should also have in it some special provision for religious action in times of frustration, disappointment and anxiety about the future. It might well also include some decision that there shall be some deliberate attention to the beauty of life, for which the imagination insatiably thirsts, and some interest in the problem of why we are here at all in this kind of a world.

There is considerable literature on the subject of the place of rule in Christian life, its usefulness and its dangers.[1] It is the easiest thing in the world to criticize the idea of living by rule and indeed to make it look ridiculous. But there is a saying of Pascal that is worth remembering. 'It is superstitious to put one's hope in formalities, but it is pride to be unwilling to submit to them.'[2] The fact is that all of us are prepared to spend unlimited time in the world of subterfuges, in hopeless fooling around on the borders of sanctity. And God must provide something to bring reality into our dream because we cannot provide this element ourselves. Rule is part of this gift of God.

But once again one comes up against the social character of the Christian religion. If we make a rule on our own and simply make a mental note of our intentions, unless we have an extraordinary willpower we shall soon forget it and content ourselves with whatever level of Christian commitment satisfied us previously. Most Christians find that they need the stimulus of a real commitment, and one made more definite by the fact that

---

[1] Martin Thornton, *Christian Proficiency*, pp. 46 ff, 62 ff.; cf. Martin Thornton, *Pastoral Theology, A Re-orientation.*

[2] *Pensées*, 249 (Everyman edition).

some other person knows what we purpose to do. It is helpful if there can be periodic check-ups with this person as to how we are holding to our chosen way of living the Christian life. This other person may be an ordained minister of the Church. It is wise to make a rule in consultation with a minister (by oneself one is bound to make it harder than one can stand) and arrange for periodic check-ups as to how things are going.

From this situation there naturally arises the use of someone as spiritual counsellor. Normally Christians find this most suitably in an ordained minister of the Church, but there is no reason preventing a layman, or laywoman, who understands the things of Christ exercising this function for someone who has his or her confidence. But there are signs that some of the traditional channels of grace in our tradition are drying up, the sermon in Sunday worship, the life of the class-meeting, the address in the weekday fellowship. There are also signs that a more intimate and personal consideration of their spiritual condition is needed today by people who want to make progress in living by faith. A minister will be the first natural choice for this help. There is no doubt that the regular use of a personal confessor and/or counsellor is one of the means by which believers are increasingly going to be helped to live the Christian life in our time. And ministers will need to be trained to exercise this personal and exacting ministry more than the preaching-visiting ministry that has been the principal part of their traditional image.[1]

It is probable that this kind of ministry will be increasingly exercised with middle-aged and older people. Young people need to be taught that Christianity is all about thankfulness and offering, that the Eucharist is the great expression of this, and that Jesus was a man with a certain attractive attitude to life in which the civilized world has maintained a continual interest and felt drawn to adopt very widely, though at the moment his friends decrease. It should be explained to them that there has not gathered round any other name in history so much created beauty, acted good, suffering gladly endured, and perhaps so much evidence of human failure, as has accumulated round the name of Jesus. They should be kept from the holy, wonder-worker, hero figure that still hovers drearily over so many

[1] Cf. the chapter 'Gurus and Guides' in *Prayer: An Adventure in Living*, B. C. Butler.

Sunday School classes and can do little but harm. As they move into adolescence it is good if they can be helped to appraise the content of the principal experiences to which human beings, in their dislike of verbal precision, attach the word 'love'. They need to learn from Christianity a sophisticated and critical attitude to the money-making and conformist world in which they live and which gets hold of us all unless we (as he said) 'watch and pray'. They need to be introduced to the civilized values. They need help in understanding what is happening in their emotional life at any given time, but only as the beginning of the task every human being has on hand all the time—to understand oneself and learn to trust one's own sincerity. They need to come to terms with the failure that runs through human relationships like a stream of tears, our rejection of the work involved in trying to understand, our shortage of mercy, pity, peace, and love. But the Christian religion can obviously be understood at any depth only in adult life, because it so obviously concerns the questions which only adults ask. Indeed, there is something rather odd and even unpleasant about a very religious child.

If we can save young people from hating the Church we have done them a great service, because the Church is somehow so hatable and they are at a time in life when the formation of the self's independence depends to some extent on having things around to which they can say their very own 'no'. The idea that all young people should be converted between the ages of 13 and 18, and that 'if we don't get them then' we never will, is ludicrous.

In the second half of the twentieth century, though the membership of the Church is formally stocked mainly from the youth-club age group, conversion is increasingly more a characteristic of middle age, when the deeper questions begin to nag at the brain.[1] Ministers may need their training switched in this direction now. It is of course admirable if a minister can be a combination of successful primary schoolteacher, scoutmaster, youth-club leader, young adults' adviser, confessor and spiritual director to those in the second half of life. But ministers do not normally come so distinguished. But it seems a lamentable affair

---

[1] Cf. an interesting article by Seward Hiltner, 'Towards a Theology of Conversion', in *Pastoral Psychology*, vol. 17. 166, pp. 35–42.

if they fail people at precisely those times when they find nudg-
ing into their minds questions as to what it is all for and why
this odd feeling of futility and precariousness just because the
youngest child has left home for his own attempt at making a
home.

Christian prayer has always been conscious of time—that
something has to be done about it to make it supportable. Time
is a continual perishing whose bitterness we cannot sweeten
merely by ignoring it or filling it full of activity to take our
minds off it. A man has to be killingly busy to keep out the
thought of death, which is just another form of the same
problem.

Christians think that time is part of the goodness of creation,
but it has been given a special holiness by the coming of Jesus
as a child of time. They believe that the way of life he commended is a way of personally experiencing the sanctification of
time. Prayer, being exercise towards this experience, takes time
seriously, indeed keeps it in the mind almost continually but
bathed in a certain sanctifying light. Morning and evening, the
week, the months and the year all influence the content and
movement of Christian prayer and so doing make themselves
felt more, not less, as part of the presence of time.[1] In this way
the passage of time is marked not just by the disappearance of
experience into nothingness but by its association with a certain
Christian mood or a related Christian belief or an event in
scripture or Christian history that sheds a special illumination
on that part of time as it recurs. This illumination is the light
of the kingdom of God as understood in the Christian religion.
Boris Pasternak said: 'Everything that happens in the world
takes place not only on the earth which buries the dead but also
in some other dimension which some call the kingdom of God.'
This Christian habit of seeing some correspondence between a
moment of time and some element of Christian experience is an
attempt to live in these two dimensions which have been joined
together by God and no one should put asunder.

Accordingly, though there is some variety in the way different
parts of Christendom have attempted the sanctification of time,
there is a wide tradition of associating Sunday with a special
dignity as the day of resurrection and therefore the day on

[1] Cf. Romano Guardini, *L'Initiation à la Prière*, pp. 41–5.

which one renews one's joy that time and death do not have the last word. There is also the custom of associating Monday in prayer with the faithful departed, Tuesday with the Holy Spirit, Wednesday with the saints, Thursday with the institution of the Eucharist and the Church's need of unity, Friday with the passion of Christ, Saturday with the Incarnation. And the months, sometimes in harmony with the movement of the natural world, have also been given special Christian associations, November with the saints and the departed, December with the word of God and the Incarnation, January with light and the appearing of the true light (in the darkest time of the year), March with the temptations of Christ, May with the Mother of our Lord, and so on.

The secular calendar blends in the Christian mind with another calendar, the liturgical calendar, which orders the basic content of Christian worship, the particular point of faith from which the Christian is called to look at his world at any given time. Christian worship is always of course the same thing, a matter of thanking God for how things are and the offering of the self to him that things may be more completely what he wills them to be. But the liturgical calendar takes the praying Christian through the principal parts of the life of Jesus and the beliefs of the Church to remind him in some detail of what we think we have most to be thankful for, and to give his praise variety of form.

This calendar certainly needs revision and is being revised in several liturgical commissions of the churches, but the revisions will simply aim at more effectively leading the praying Christian through the due subjects of a Christian attention, so that he may relate these to the life he is living and the world in which he is living it. According to this presentation of time, the weeks of Advent and Christmas concern the coming of Christ, the Epiphany weeks concern his baptism and ministry, the Lenten weeks his interior life and his sufferings, Easter his resurrection and triumph, Pentecost the Holy Spirit and the Church; the weeks following concern the Christian beliefs about the being of God, the sacraments, Christian life and witness, the communion of saints and the life everlasting, after which, with Advent, the annual survey of Christian basic conviction begins again.

In this way, Christians have traditionally attempted to make process meaningful by relating its fleeting moments with that which abides in Christian memory and Christian understanding of life. It is still the standard means by which believers learn 'to weave a continuous thread of the spiritual and supernatural through the quotidian homespun, and ennoble the whole of life with a hieratic dignity'.[1]

---

[1] Patrick L. Fermor, *Mani*, p. 219. The development of the Christian idea of 'the sanctification of time' is considered in *The Shape of the Liturgy*: Dom Gregory Dix, ch. 11.

13

When it is Impossible to Pray

QUITE often people who have not yet come to faith have an anticipatory understanding that prayer is at the heart of religion. They secretly envy people who pray, and they vaguely want to pray themselves. If they come to faith they find that, in the Christian understanding of the matter, to want to pray is in fact to have arrived and that many Christians many times in their lives do not have much more to offer God than the desire to offer. When we find it impossible to pray but at the back of the mind is the struggling wish that we could, the presence is with us. 'Console thyself, thou wouldst not seek Me if thou hadst not found Me.'[1]

The life of faith often begins in this suspicious, tentative groping that mysteriously insists on being taken seriously. When Charles de Foucauld, in the sophisticated and somewhat chaotic life he was living during his period of military service, began to feel the old dissatisfaction that a million times in human experience has announced the need of some inner reorganization, he began to drop in to churches as he passed by them. He was surprised to find himself peculiarly at ease there, and only there; and he would spend some time there repeating one short prayer: 'My God, if you exist, make me know you.'

Among people feeling the very first interest in religion there may be a state prior to this when even this is not possible. The self that wants God intuitively suspects that a part of it must die if it is going to get what it wants, and so it resists and evades, finds all things connected with formal committed religion appalling, but it thirsts still. In this situation people should not attempt any kind of formal prayer, certainly not read any literature in the subject, and avoid all church buildings, but simply, as often during the day as they care, say something

[1] Pascal, *Pensées* (Everyman edition), 552.

in the de Foucauld manner like 'O God, if you exist, draw me
to you'.

But it is not surprising that de Foucauld resorted to church
buildings in his desperation. Among all the many kinds of holiness there is a holiness of place. And this is not confined to
Christianity. Any place where men and women have persistently
prayed has a differentiating atmosphere which is conducive to
prayer. Anyone who has visited the classical Greek religious
centre at Paestum in Italy, its three pre-Christian temples
standing there still, their tutelary gods mysteriously present as
vanished presences, knows the peculiarly stabilizing power of
this atmosphere. So Philip Larkin writes in his poem 'Church-
going':[1]

> For, though I've no idea
> What this accoutred frowsty barn is worth,
> It pleases me to stand in silence here;
>
> A serious house on serious earth it is,
> In whose blent air all our compulsions meet,
> Are recognised, and robed as destinies.
> And that much never can be obsolete,
> Since someone will forever be surprising
> A hunger in himself to be more serious,
> And gravitating with it to this ground,
> Which, he once heard, was proper to grow wise in,
> If only that so many dead lie round.

It has always been part of the Christian idea that faith is a
gift of God, therefore conferring no merit or superiority on him
who believes (because God pours his sunshine on saint and
criminal with the same irrational generosity), and consequently
to be asked for in prayer. It is good to make this request in some
place built by faith and for faith and frequented by faith. Conceivably some of this faith might brush off on the seeker who,
hesitantly at first, then with a gathering hope, turns aside from
his world into this world and says, if only to himself, that he
wants to believe in God and understand what Christians mean
by this famous word.

Oddly enough it is possible to feel the attraction of prayer
more strongly than that of belief. It is a not uncommon ex-

[1] In *Contemporary Verse* (Penguin Books), p. 337.

perience today but it is a risky one and can lead people a long way from Christianity—into vague religiosity, occultism, and superstition. In its Christian use, praying is inseparable from Christian thought about God. 'For it would seem clear that no one can call upon Thee without knowing Thee, for if he did he might invoke another than Thee, knowing Thee not . . . let me utter my prayer believing in Thee: for Thou hast been preached to us.'[1] But the honest man who wishes to pray but whose mind seizes up before this fact, before the fact that prayer is to the Father through the Son in the Holy Spirit, can take another road.

It is to concentrate on the equally close connection between praying and loving in the mind of Jesus. It is not that he should not pray *until* he has been reconciled to his brother, or to life itself, but that prayer and reconciliation are, in the Christian view, extremely closely connected and certainly mutually in-fluential. If he cannot pray, he can prepare the way by making some attempt at reconciling himself with his brother, his col-leagues, wife, his past, life itself. He can concern himself with such examples of human need or human injustice of which his daily experience makes him aware. All this effort may well bring him to the most acute realization of his need of the power of God, if such power exists, and therefore so near the edge of prayer that he may quite easily fall in. The attempt to live by such moral conviction as we have can bring us into a mental condition in which the Christian interpretation of life seems much more reasonable. The New Testament way of putting this is the idea that the moral law is like the servant who in the ancient world accompanied the child to school—school being (in this context) the place where one learns to understand life and its contents, and used as an image for Christ himself.

Then there is the realm of the beautiful, the experiences in which we enjoy, admire and are thankful for those things which men by some untraceable inspiration or some fantastic fluke have created to form that storehouse of joy that is the world of art. Enjoyment of this range of experience is sometimes dis-missed by the earnest as mere aestheticism and pejoratively set against the experience of God's love in redemption. This con-trast does not spring from a Christian understanding of life.

---

[1] St. Augustine, *Confessions* (trans. F. J. Sheed), p. 1.

Both experiences are the place of God's revealing of himself. The fundamentalist cannot deny that in scripture we are exhorted to attend to whatsoever things are lovely. Some people need no exhortation, some do. The latter are generally those who forget that the Christian Church has always felt a little shaky about the doctrine of redemption and has never bound its members to any one theory of the atonement whilst it has always been certain of its conception of the Holy Spirit as the creative and life-giving presence of God. We would not have been exhorted to attend to the beautiful unless it was believed that the presence of God is there. And in the Christian view, the person contemplating the proportion and skilful arrangement of forms by which the eye is gratifyingly carried up, down, across a picture and in this way given that satisfaction that is so commonly known yet so defiant of analysis is concerned with the being and purpose of God, as is the scholar, the lover, the philosopher, the politician, the teacher, in his own realm of experience.

The person who cannot 'pray' may yet be able to live intensively in the world of thanking. This is half of what Christian prayer is about, though initially we do not realize this and do not realize that there is someone to thank. It is worth while frequently considering in remembrance of things past the occasions which, if we were believers, we might well call signs of the presence of God. It would amount to the pleasant task of enumerating our moments of greatest happiness, but it would not stop there; we know that some stretches of experience which were all curses and gloom have turned out to be very different from what they seemed, have been seen in a later light to be contributors to our life and not thieves of it.

Certainly believers themselves need more trustingly to give the name of God to more tracts of experience than they are accustomed to glorify in this way. And this must be one of the marks of spiritual growth—to see God, or suspect the presence of God, in more places than we did, say, three years ago. It could be one of the forms of taking the name of God in vain (when 'name' equals 'presence' whether consciously named or not) to accept life and enjoy it without being willing to call any of it God. Conversely, another form would be doing things, say, in the life of the Church, which are now spent and irrelevant, continuing to do them simply because we have grown accustomed to name the name of God over them and think this custom itself makes what we are doing his will.

It is part of the teaching of Simone Weil that there is such a thing as the 'implicit love of God', experiences in which God is present though unrealized by the person involved in the experience. These experiences are those which are constituted by the apprehension of the beauty of the world, the love of our neighbour, and participation in the orthodox religious acts of the worshipping Church.[1] 'They do not disappear when the love of God in the full sense of the word wells up in the soul; they become infinitely stronger, and all loves taken together only make a single love.'[2] She argues, as we have seen, that within the love of the beauty of the world is hidden the longing for the Incarnation. Everyone who enjoys the beauty of the world ultimately longs for it to be embodied in a person. And all the diverse kinds of vice are essentially distorted longings for that experience in which the beauty of the world becomes tangible.[3] But he whom we acknowledge to be master has said 'Do not touch me'. There is an ultimate joy which Christians believe to be not possible in this world, indeed not legitimate. But 'after this exile' eye hath not seen nor ear heard nor has it entered into the imagination of man the things that God has prepared for them that love him. The Christian view is that the experience of the beautiful does not contain in itself any finality, it inevitably leaves a certain dissatisfaction and restlessness in the mind, and this will be allayed only after death, in the glory to be revealed then. Nevertheless he who loves the beauty of the world and the realm of beautiful artefacts must be, though he may not realize it, loving and praising God.

Some people find it impossible to pray because they think it indicates presumption on their part. In one way this is a healthy reaction from the cosy and intimate relationship with God purveyed by some evangelical pleaders who sell religion warm and cheap; but it can also be an exaggeration of reverence before God which takes people out of the truth. If God is what the great Christian creeds say he is, if he is anything like the Holy

[1] Simone Weil, *Waiting on God* (Routledge and Kegan Paul), pp. 81 ff.
[2] Op. cit., p. 82.
[3] Simone Weil, op. cit., p. 110.

Trinity, it is natural and right to wonder how he can possibly be interested in me. But it has been pointed out that behind this way of thinking is the conviction that one 'lowers oneself' by attending to smaller fry than one considers oneself to be.[1] This is an extremely human way of thinking about God, drawn from the hierarchical world of commerce where the managing director is spared encounters with staff personnel 'at the bottom' who do not count for much, his time being so devastatingly valuable that his secretary makes appointments for him only with very important people. To transfer this ludicrously human way of thinking into one's understanding of the being of God is one of the forms of blasphemy. God, thank God, is not some dreadful managing director, or, as Blake said 'an allegory of kings, and nothing else', who only sees important people, he is revealed in Jesus Christ who says when some unknown woman tries to get near him, 'Who touched me?', that is to say, 'Who was it in this mass of indifferent, casual, curious humanity who really wanted me?'

People find it impossible to pray when their idea of God has not been modified by experience and adult reflection but has remained at a childish level, perhaps that at which their last contact with the Church left them. They know that this is a childish concept of God and in their maturity they cannot pray to it. Though they have not thought the matter through they know they simply do not believe in that kind of a God now. This seems to happen frequently. Therefore it is wise for the Church to allow for it and not teach its young people anything which in later life they must *repudiate*. It is one thing to teach ideas of God to which deeper thoughts can be added, it is another and quite unjustifiable matter to teach ideas of God which the growing mind must necessarily discard as part of the toys of childhood or despise if for some reason it cannot discard them.

People often say they find it impossible to pray when, as they put it, they have 'lost their faith'. But there is usually some confusion about this situation. Faith is not a thing one can lose, like a purse or a ring of keys.[2] When people speak about losing their faith what generally has happened is that they have for some time not been thinking about their life in terms of their

[1] Cf. Jacques Rivière, À *la Trace de Dieu*, pp. 51-4.
[2] Cf. Georges Bernanos, *The Diary of a Country Priest* (Fontana), pp. 105-6.

faith, they have not been living by it; and this is precisely the result of ceasing to pray as Christianity understands prayer. The less we pray, the less we experience life in the Christian way. We move into another mental world. Even so, other kinds of prayer may well be possible there, some intellectually defensible, some not. We all pray in one way or another far more than we think.

It is certain that genuine intellectual perplexity will disturb any routine adopted for maintaining and deepening Christian faith. This perplexity may be due to difficulty in understanding what prayer is and how to use it; this difficulty is widespread, and we simply must pray the Holy Spirit to help us to understand prayer more fully and to help one another in the Church to understand. But the problem of belief that stops prayer may be more general and amount to a Christian's questioning any kind of religious interpretation of life. This could be the prelude to a definite conscious repudiation of the faith, in which case, of course, the Christian use of prayer will cease.

But the turmoil of intellectual perplexity can often be misinterpreted. A time may come when we cannot think of any part of the faith without questioning it, and yet, far from this indicating that our faith is in danger, it shows that it is very much alive.

There will always be something we do not understand and something to criticize in the Christian faith as we attempt to live it, but there are certain times when questions and criticisms dominate the mind. These are usually times of psychological change when the self is moving to a new level of maturity and undergoing the necessary process of disintegration and reforming; for example, during adolescence, at the achievement of adulthood, at the transition to the second half of life, at retirement from full participation in the working life of the community. All these are periods of complex challenge, fear, hope and regret. As each is successfully negotiated the personality is to some extent re-born.

Our faith has also on each occasion to undergo some re-birth, it must grow so that our Christian thought about life matches the way we are experiencing it now. The lapse of many confirmed Christians at the end of their teens, when they leave school for their first job or for some form of further education, is frequently to be traced to their realization how infantile their youth-club brand of faith looks now and how useless it is in the world in which they currently find themselves living. The religious doubts and questionings that come at these times are signs of health, of the self's irritation with what it understands religion to be and its determination to finish with it unless it can find a Christian understanding of life that it can respect for its present value.

If these critical times of change are to be times of spiritual advance there is no way round the necessary work. There is thinking and reading to be done, we should ask for help from those we think can help us, we should hold on to such minimal conviction and religious practice as still have a trace of meaning for us, and we should trust that we shall be led out into the light again. Part of the classical Christian notion of faith is that it is not only a gift but a virtue, and this is because faith is so closely related to the life of the will. Certainly obedience and perseverance have always been far more familiar ingredients of faith than have emotional transports of one kind and another. Evangelists have tended to betray their hearers by commending the faith in too lively a fashion. Christian faith is not easy, it is not always hugely interesting, it rarely produces immediate results (how could it? It is a learned life not a washing powder,) and it must change with the growing self.

The 20-year-old either takes his religion into all the crucial living he is going through, accepting that *it* will be changed with so much else that is changing for him, or else he leaves it on the shores of youth as the tide of life moves out to greater depths. Many people do leave it there, and when later they want a faith they go back looking for this bit of their youth, only to find it now a dreadful embarrassment. A faith is useless out of its time.

The degree of pain in these critical experiences must obviously vary with the circumstances and temperament of the person concerned. When it is severe it may be quite impossible to pray. Contrary to the popular criticism of Christianity that it is resorted to primarily for comfort by those in trouble, the truth is that most people find that gloom drives them from God not to him and that it is always easiest to pray when one is happy. Accordingly in times of intense emotional complexity or the periods of spiritual listlessness which have always been a trouble to earnest Christians, there may be little to do other than endure and make some attempt to reduce one's self-absorption. It is good not to take oneself too seriously and to realize that when life is lived by faith it has the same rhythm of change from darkness to light and back which any life has, which the life of the natural world has. It is sensible then to make more use of the sacramental life of the Church in whose objectivity and doctrinal fullness it is easier to 'lift up our hearts' to God and get away from ourselves. These times also prove the value of having variety in one's praying routines and programmes, and of making full use of many different sources of spiritual re-assurance—in the world of art, literature, music, recreation. Many people become bored with prayer simply because they do the same thing interminably.[1]

Prayer is difficult in certain other contexts of self-preoccupation. The person who is apparently negotiating life's problems with some success and is steadily mounting the ladder of promotion in the world of his daily work is liable to develop an olympian omnicompetence which finds the religious dimension of life increasingly irrelevant. In this atmosphere prayer dies. While we are self-sufficient we do not want God.

Another kind of self-sufficiency can develop for the opposite reason. Many people feel keenly that they have not much to show for their lives; nevertheless this self is them, it is their small bit of identity and value. But the less confident you are about yourself the more you protect it, and the less free you are to *give* it to anyone or anything. Similarly the idea of God's omni-science is devastating for such people; the thought that someone knows us utterly in his all-embracing comprehension takes from them the last vestige of their individuality. For such people to bring God into their lives, to give themselves to God is not really possible. They already experience life too much as a threatening affair and so, with an exaggerated passion, they desire to hang on to this self that counts for so little but is at least 'me'. To bring God in, they feel, would be to lose all, in some sense go under in some sea of impossible obligations and claims. Prayer is not possible for a person who is too insecure to trust, unless God gives this grace, and he certainly does not give it always.

---

[1] Cf. Von Hugel, *The Life of Prayer*, pp. 33–8.

And the other principal self-preoccupation is guilt. To pray in the Christian way means a criticism and purification and reorganization of our desires. If this exercise throws exposing light on some area of our lives which we know to be against the will of God and therefore presents us again and again with the need for change there it becomes unbearable. We either make the necessary change or we stop praying. Actually there is no need to stop praying, and many people in this situation do not find it impossible to pray. There are many Christians who have simply expressed to God their honest conflict of wanting him but not on his terms, wanting release from sin but not yet,[1] and this seems a reasonable thing to do—to tell God how discreditably it is with us. If we can pray only when we are virtuous we shall never pray at all.

The situation that is most likely to turn us against God and the Christian understanding that life is lived within a loving providence is the experience of disaster. This stops prayer as frequently as any other experience. But here again it is still possible to pray though we ourselves may not be people who can pray under such strain. There is a long tradition of prayer as argument with God. The book of Job is really an account of a man's dialogue with God, even his fight with God, in the experience of disaster. The prayer of Jesus on the cross is the archetypal cry of dismay at God's ways. Wesley's hymn on the theme of wrestling Jacob, in its full version, is an account of a man's inner argument with God on the question of who he (God) is—whether it is love or hate or indifference that directs our existence. Much of the writing of Dostoevsky can be interpreted similarly as a prolonged argument with God as to whether he is entitled to the name of love. François Mauriac points out that Baudelaire, in his chaotic life, however much he denied, never really ceased to pray. He was always addressing the reality of this world, with whom he knew from a very early age that he had a peculiar relationship of belonging and disinheritance.[2] The novelist Tolstoy and the poet Dylan Thomas had a similar relationship of struggle with God. Indeed this situation is extremely common in Christian history. The prayer of question and accusation and even hostility to God is genuine

[1] St. Augustine, *Confessions* (Everyman Edition), p. 163.
[2] François Mauriac, *Mémoires Intérieures*, p. 50.

prayer, it is a religious movement of the mind, it is a long way from the characteristic Christian prayer of thanking and self-offering, but it is genuine, and true to a certain stage in the search for God and truth. And there are people who spend their whole life in this condition. Because of circumstantial or temperamental factors religion is an endless struggle and argument for them, with no sign of help in sight, certainly not from the Church. 'And Jacob was left alone; and there wrestled a man with him until the breaking of the day.' It is true that we are nearest to God when we are loving him, but we are certainly very close when we are fighting him.

Often when people cannot pray they can at least act, just as often when they cannot act they can at least pray. Life is not all thought; and when some shock has expelled from our minds all that we have received from the Church (and hitherto believed) about God, the longing for truth and such belief in loving as still survive within us can express themselves in action that is at any rate directed towards making things better for the world and not worse. There is a fine passage in Albert Camus's *The Plague* in which the priest, Paneloux, and the unbelieving doctor, Rieux, find a point of existence at which they can virtually stand hand in hand:

(The priest has just been speaking about 'grace'.) Rieux had sunk back again on the bench. His lassitude had returned and from its depths he spoke, more gently.

'It's something I haven't got; that I know. But I'd rather not discuss that with you. We're working side by side for something that unites us—beyond blasphemy and prayers. And it's the only thing that matters.'

Paneloux sat down beside Rieux. It was obvious that he was deeply moved.

'Yes, yes,' he said, 'you too are working for man's salvation.'

Rieux tried to smile.

'Salvation's much too big a word for me. I don't aim so high. I'm concerned with man's health, and for me his health comes first. . . . What I hate is death and disease—as you well know. And whether you wish it or not, we're allies, facing them and fighting them together.' Rieux was still holding Paneloux's hand. 'So you see'—but he refrained from meeting the priest's eyes—'God himself can't part us now.'[1]

[1] Albert Camus, *The Plague* (Penguin Edition), pp. 178–9.

Finally, when it is impossible to pray it is still possible to be silent before God and experience. The value of silence may have to be learned, especially by fellowships that have developed round the theology of the word. In the traditional language of Christian religion there repeatedly comes the phrase 'waiting on God'. It is one of the ways of saying that if, in the attitude of faith, you are willing to silence the egoistical monologue that goes so dreadfully on in the mind and prevents you understanding and appreciating both the world outside and your inner, and most important, self, you will become aware of a deeper self which is more truly you than the superficial self that incessantly shouts its likes and dislikes. This deeper self again and again is found to have an authority that more clearly voices your inner life than more frequently encountered moods or aspects of the self, simply because there has been a silence and a waiting and a permission for this self to speak.

And Methodists who have learned so much from the life of the word, from divine and human self-communication in stating, questioning, protesting, confessing, have perhaps to learn now that there are gifts to be received in the world of silence, from that disposition of the mind which forsakes the word and simply waits in the presence, in the present situation which *is* the presence of God and waits therefore expectantly. The work of Simone Weil, especially her books *Waiting on God* and *Gravity and Grace*,[1] and her concept of prayer as essentially the purest form of *attention* indicate certainly one of the ways of thinking which our tradition has lacked too long.

There are situations which are so charged with joy or pain that there is nothing to *say*. In the painful situation we can at least be still, waiting for life to unfold itself, dropping rigidity and defensiveness, not imposing our will on experience but ready for all his perfect will who is the way and truth and life. This is a truly Christian use of praying, but silence is an essential part of it. The silence required is not only outer quiet but inward tranquillity too—the silencing of the self-centred monologue of aggression or withdrawal that perpetually flows through the mind. Whilst we are carried along on the surface of this stream of egoism we are not really living, we do not know the truth about the world around us or our own deepest desires, we

[1] Published by Routledge and Kegan Paul (the former also in Fontana Books).

do not live authentically—in touch with the real world and our real self, we live a phoney existence constructed out of our fears and hates and compensating dreams. And it never enters our heads that the truth could be much more pleasant than this agitated fantasy we build as a retreat from it.

So, generally speaking, when we cannot pray by ourselves we should certainly hold more securely to those occasions when we pray with the worshipping Church. This is in any case the primary context of Christian prayer, and it may be the only one in which prayer is possible for many Christians, though they must in this way necessarily live an incomplete spiritual life.

If this becomes impossible too there is nothing for it but to frequent as much as possible those areas of experience which religious man has consistently thought to be forms of the presence of God, and as many of them as possible. We must direct our living to enjoying the beautiful, looking for the truth (worth while even about trivialities), practising liking human beings (they are not liked enough, certainly not as much as they deserve), bringing some understanding and reliable love into the lonely muddle that life is for so many people, attempting to understand oneself (though one cannot get far in this important pursuit alone), and simply waiting for the return of what Christians call grace. If we are living in these realms of experience, rejecting pride, we are where the Presence is and we are loving. It does not matter if we cannot identify him or find words to say to him for the time being.

14

The Night of Faith

THE Christian believes that life is to be lived by faith. Accordingly, our day-to-day assurance is one of trust, not perception. It is doubtful whether we should ever ask for the *sense* of God's presence, or that we may be made *very conscious* of his presence, though innumerable services and meetings have begun with such petitions in our tradition for years.

If we are agreed that we live by faith, the request for such favours is scarcely Christian. It is more like Orpheus wanting to look round and see if his Eurydice is really there.

One of the classical ideas in the literature of Christian prayer is that of the dark night of the soul. Many people seem to think of this phrase a meaning some mysterious agony that comes to religious people; and it is often used, quite illegitimately, as a metaphor for particular periods of gloom in the religious life. The phrase was not so used by its originator, St. John of the Cross.

It appears that for St. John of the Cross the image of 'the dark night' was in the first instance simply the most accurate one he could find for the ordinary life of faith. He chose it because when he thought about the life of faith he was much impressed with the fact that sense-impressions have so little to do with normal experience of God as Christians understand it.

In *The Ascent of Mount Carmel* St. John of the Cross gives three reasons why the image of a dark night is useful for the life of faith.[1]

The first is that God is spirit, and among the various meanings of this term is the idea that, as Christians understand him, there is nothing in God on which our senses can operate. He is spiritually, not sensibly or sensually, experienced. Any experience in which there is nothing to engage our senses must be of the same kind as a dark night is to the sense of sight, as silence

---

[1] Cf. St. John of the Cross, *Ascent of Mt. Carmel*, Book 1, ch. 2. 1.

148

is to the sense of hearing, as immateriality is to the sense of touch, and so on. The idea of a dark night is a strictly visual metaphor, but St. John makes it clear that he uses it to convey the uselessness not only of the sense of sight but of all the senses in the life of faith.

The second reason for St. John's choice of the image of the dark night is that our ignorance of God is stupendous. God is the infinitely transcendent mystery, he is in fact a whole dark night in himself. It is questionable that we know anything of him apart from that which we believe he has revealed of himself. And such revelation of himself as he has given can only be as much of himself as our finite minds can understand. The more that he must be begins to tantalize the mind as it fumbles for words that are not in any dictionary. Of course, Jesus Christ, we believe, has humanized God for us, so that it is much easier for people who have 'seen' Jesus to love God than for others. But there is a mystery about Jesus too. No one seems to understand him in any final and complete way, the scholars present a different view of him in almost every generation, it is still true that, as Schweitzer said, he comes to us as 'one unknown, without a name, as of old by the lakeside, he came to those men who knew him not'.[1]

Finally, St. John reminds us of the simple truth that faith is not knowledge. Faith is a risky affair, a journey into the unknown. You may believe that you have a guide, but he has the map, not you. Even when you think you can see a bit of the way ahead there may be a sudden pull on your sleeve, a disconcerting change of direction. There are the many contradictions and incongruities of the journey. So much of life simply does not make sense at all. It is better to settle for the word 'believe'. Christians are ill at ease with the word 'know', except in the sentence 'I know whom I have believed'.

And so St. John sees the Christian as rather like a blind man, taking faith alone for guide and light, and in the last resort finding little use in things he understands, feels, imagines, as he makes his journey in God and to God. The world of faith is a colourless, silent world, perhaps some people might call it bleak. When you get into it, if you are a person of normal emotional response, you cannot help hoping that at some turn of the

[1] A. Schweitzer, *The Quest of the Historical Jesus*, p. 401.

road a match will be struck unexpectedly in the dark, lighting up some friendly presence, or at least something of the way ahead.

According to St. John this does happen sometimes. It happens at the beginning of the life of faith. There is the vivid joy of conversion, the peace that comes when we stop fighting God and life, the feeling of strength and well-being which floods the self when debilitating doubts have given way to genuine convictions. Even those who experience little of this pleasure feel on conversion an exhilarating decisiveness about life and find it easy to pray and go to church.

But it does not last. And it was never meant to last.

Because our emotional life is so important to us, it seems that God has to start there. He has to confirm our new-found interest in the kingdom which is not of this world by surrounding that interest, initially, with a bit of this-worldly pleasure. Otherwise we would never make a start on the life of faith at all. But nothing is more certain than that this pleasure, peace, joy, conviction is soon going to be withdrawn. Religious experience will then seem to be singularly devoid of signs or favours of an emotional nature.

For these reasons the life of faith must *normally* seem like going on a silent journey through a dark night. And when the excitement and pleasure of our first commitment to God vanish, we can say: 'This is it; this is the end of the beginning. Now I have really begun the Christian life.'

It appears that the other time when the thrills come is when the Christian has travelled a very long way in the spiritual life, when he has made the extremely demanding progress in humility and detachment which characterizes the life of the saint. The saint's intense, single-minded love of God engages his whole being, including his emotional nature. In the wholeness of sanctification the response of the feelings can at last be trusted to be an unequivocal response to God. But all this is just about as relevant to our spiritual journey as details of the weather on the top of Everest are to someone climbing the Downs.

The general idea in Christian teaching about prayer is that pleasant feelings may well come at the beginning of the life of commitment. It is not an inevitable experience but it is a frequent one at that stage. It has traditionally been regarded in the same category as rewards for children when we want to encourage their moral growth; parents soon withdraw the inducements and expect the growing child to do kind acts without thinking of reward. The Christian has to expect a similar withdrawal of favours in his spiritual growth, and fairly soon if he is in earnest. When he reaches this point, and finds that serving God is beginning to seem a rather cold and dark affair he can be assured that nothing is wrong, indeed all is right, and he has now, and only now, really begun the life of *faith*.

In the light of this teaching many popular religious difficulties disappear. One is the common feeling that 'no one is there' when one is praying. This is not a difficulty; it is normal and right to feel that no one is there when one is praying. The Holy Trinity is not *a person*.

Another difficulty is the absence of any sense of communion, or even of devout feeling at all, at Holy Communion. This makes people think that they are just acting a part. Because they sense (feel) nothing, they consider the whole thing senseless (meaningless). Nothing could be farther from the truth. The experience may well be senseless, but it is not therefore meaningless. On St. John's principles, it could be argued that, given a good intention, the less feeling there is in religious experience the more meaningful it is.

Then there is the state of boredom with religion, with church services, religious literature, the practice of prayer, which attacks the Christian for whom the aura of conversion has begun to wear off. It is responsible for a great deal of disillusion and backsliding. The voice of the spirit that speaks through hundreds of years of Christian sanctity suggests we are fools to become agitated about this, because it is on the way to every believer as soon as he starts ignoring his feelings and tries living by faith.

St. Teresa makes this comment on this situation: 'But when I hear servants of God, men of weight, learning and understanding, worrying so much because he is not giving them devotion, it makes me sick to listen to them. I do not say that they should not accept it if God grants it to them, and value it too . . . but they should not be distressed when they do not receive it. They should realize that since the Lord does not give it to them they do not need it. They should exercise control over themselves and go right ahead.'[1]

There is much to be said for the deliberate renunciation of the desire for 'consolations' (the word traditionally used in Christian spirituality for the awareness of God's action in the mind when that action is comforting). The orthodox position is not as extreme as that. It is that we are to be thankful for such spiritual comfort when it comes and not perturbed when it goes. But there is considerable evidence for the view that, in prayer, awareness of God is infrequent. In addition to his own vast knowledge of the literature of the subject, Dom John Chapman discussed the life of prayer with many men and women of prayer throughout his life. He makes this interesting comment:

> I fancy that the majority of those religious of both sexes who practise contemplative prayer would be likely to state that they have no perception whatever of God's presence or of his existence, though they are conscious of an intense desire of him and sometimes an intense love. . . . (They) would probably say that they rather want him than perceive him, that they are more conscious of his absence than his presence, and would put down their certainty of him to reason and to faith, more than to perception or consciousness.[2]

If that kind of spiritual experience is at all common, the widespread assumption that religion will bring much 'sensible' consolation is extremely misleading. It must take thousands of people annually into severe disappointment, if not into disillusion. It is not a bad policy therefore to move towards the other extreme, to lean over backwards a little and assume that there will probably be no sense of Presence most of the time. Chapman often gave exactly this advice:

> 'So we must aim at being in the desert . . . and not at any consciousness of God's grace and presence. One is inclined to say "I am so weak, I can't go on like this! I must have some consolation, or I shall merely fall and grow worldly". But God knows best. Absolute and complete confidence, trust, abandon, is what we need.'[3]

[1] St. Teresa, *Life* (Tr. J. M. Cohen), ch. 11.
[2] Dom John Chapman, *Spiritual Letters*, p. 312.
[3] Dom John Chapman, *Spiritual Letters*, p. 173.

'You are on the look out for "consolation", merely because you still imagine that you are not serving God properly when you are in dryness. Make up your mind once for all that dryness is best, and you will find that you are frightened at having anything else!'[1]

But there are certain assurances commonly met with in the dark journey of faith. There are journeying mercies for even the phlegmatic.

When Jesus said, 'If I by the finger of God cast out devils, then is the kingdom of God come upon you', he had in mind a deliverance which some people he believed had already experienced and others would. If the word 'deliverance' means anything at all it may be expected to trail a sense of relief as it comes upon you. If the words 'kingdom of God' hold any of the meanings assigned to them in the Christian religion, the coming of God's rule into one's life must be noticeable, perhaps not always immediately by other people but certainly by oneself, and after the first enthusiasms have cooled down. If the rule of God within one's life is signified by the 'fruits of the spirit', the nine presences or forms of the Presence so admirably listed by St. Paul,[2] faith must begin to have a little supporting knowledge to make the night a little less dark. Some of this experience is for ordinary Christian sinners. The flowers are not for only the canonized to pick.

There is a certain task of identification. This takes time. Some assurances cannot come at once because they come on the back of a great quantity of lived life. Whilst we are fighting our passage through, the presence of God may seem infinitely distant, but there are times when as we pause to look back things have a remarkable way of falling into a pattern, as though some creative grace was present all along. The experience which seemed intolerable or pointless when it was present is now set in a past which has the surprising look of meaning which awakens thankfulness. Christians have learned to trust the evidence supplied by this backward look over the journey; it is indeed a feature of biblical religion, particularly of the spirituality of the psalms.

It has been pointed out that, in any case, there can hardly be

[1] Op. cit., p. 99.
[2] Epistle to the Galatians, v. 22–3.

an awareness of *present* experience of God. Being who he is, he must, if we are aware of him, at least take our eyes off ourselves for once, give us a taste of self-forgetfulness.

> One can only speak of the knowledge of God in the past tense or in the future tense because the present tense, which would be knowing God consciously here and now, would take one entirely out of oneself and . . . leave one with nothing to say. In practice, therefore, to know God is to look back and to look forward and to live now in the light of the looking back, and in the light of the looking forward. I *have* known God, for there has been kindled in me that which I can recognise in the history . . . of the people of God. So there is also the looking forward. Because I have known God I am certain that I *shall* know God. . . . Doubts which come to one in the middle of the fact that one has known God, in the sure and certain hope that one will know God, are simply challenges to enter more fully into the meaning of belief.[1]

Along with this awareness of the providence of God many believers come to a point when they know that their day-to-day handling of life is more affectionate and less agitated than it was before they began the life of Christian commitment. People must naturally vary considerably in this, some being clearly convinced of it, others only prepared to say they think it may well be so; and all who belong to a Christian tradition that has a deep concern about the inward realities of faith will be aware of the dangers of spiritual pride and of the ease with which human beings are deceived about their condition. Even so, the awareness of improvement in coping with existence, certainly of increased happiness about being alive in this kind of a world, has always been part of the Christian experience.

It is sometimes argued that this could be simply the result of the normal process of maturing; a believer of 30 years of age who has negotiated successfully such experiences as qualifying in his chosen trade or profession, his first opportunities of promotion, marriage and the establishing of a home and family, will naturally have a poise and assurance he did not have ten years ago. That is true, but, as Christians understand it, spiritual progress is not the same thing as psychological growth, though they must exercise a mutual influence. It is particularly a matter of progress in loving, and loving life, persons and things. It is

[1] D. E. Jenkins, *Jesus and God*, pp. 84-5.

often not difficult to distinguish the assurance that is due to psychological growth, professional success and recognition[1] from that which is due to being kept in the knowledge and love of God and of his son Jesus Christ. And even when this distinction is not clear, the fact remains that one of the principal results of the Christian use of praying is that one is increasingly disinclined to separate nature and grace, one interprets life as a whole, and thankfully as coming from God. Christians think it is God who urges them to persist in doing this.

In the varieties of Christian experience, as we have seen, there are examples of an immediate assurance of God's presence, or at any rate as soon as the mind has found the power to reflect on it, which must of course be much more vivid than the conviction that grows retrospectively over the years. The classical teaching is that these moments may occur at the very beginning of the life of commitment and when the believer has gone a very long way along the path of holiness.

But there must be occasions, between these two extremes, when a sudden experience of release or illumination may fill one's being with a joy which one naturally refers to God. Wesley's experience in Aldersgate Street (which Methodism has so over-cooked as to make it almost unpalatable) was clearly such a special moment of release, the finding of a new depth of understanding, during his journey of faith.

Pascal's experience on the night of 23rd November 1654 which he recounted in his infinitely moving *Memorial*[2] is another and more eloquent and realistic example of this range of experience.[3] Yet another is that of Simone Weil, reciting to herself George Herbert's poem 'Love bade me welcome'.[4]

Experiences as vivid as these must be exceptional. Wesley certainly spoke cautiously about his own, perhaps realizing what a heady doctrine enthusiasm could brew out of it. He contended that those who teach that no one has saving faith who has not the witness of the Spirit do not 'speak the truth as it is in Jesus'. Indeed, he had reservations even about 'the con-

[1] Cf. '. . . on whom assurance sits As a silk hat on a Bradford millionaire'— T. S. Eliot, *The Waste Land*, 233–4.
[2] Pascal, *Pensées* (trans. Krailsheimer), no. 913.
[3] Cuthbert Butler, *Western Mysticism* (Grey Arrow Books), pp. 74–5.
[4] Simone Weil, *Waiting on God* (Kegan Paul), p. 21.

sciousness of being in the favour of God' (an expression he seems
to have preferred to the word 'assurance'):

> I believe the consciousness of being in the favour of God . . . is
> the common privilege of Christians fearing God and working
> righteousness. Yet I do not affirm that there are no exceptions to
> this general rule. Possibly some may be in the favour of God, and
> yet go mourning all the day long. But I believe this is usually
> owing either to disorder of body or ignorance of the gospel pro-
> mises. Therefore I have not for many years thought a conscious-
> ness of acceptance to be essential to justifying faith.[1]

What most people find in the Christian religion, if they learn
and live the life of faith within the prayer of the Church, and
earnestly (because it all matters to them personally), is quite
simply an increase of happiness. If, when sin is confessed, we
have peace with God, if each eucharist is both his presence and
the anticipation of the feast that awaits us when earth's time has
run out, if faith introduces us to a dimension of life in which
this world's horrors can be met creatively, such good things
must necessarily give people a happiness they never knew before
they turned to the life of faith. And these things are merely part
of, they do not exhaust, the persisting and cumulative effects of
living by faith. And the Christian refers it all to the presence of
God. He could be fantastically wrong. But this is in fact how
Christians live life. The assurance of God's presence will vary in
intensity for different people, and at different times for the same
person, and sometimes it will be completely obscured. But that
life is good and that it is good to live it this way and that it is
good because it is lived this way is the common Christian conviction. Christians are not alone in finding life good of course.
But all the others who do so are at liberty to shout too.

Yet the Christian life is so much more than assurances that
any protracted attention to them upsets the balance of things.
The balance is restored by Christian teaching on the sanctification of life. Indeed, these two Christian elements, the awareness
of God's favour and the call to the heights of loving, really
belong together. Either in isolation from the other is a menace.

Towards the end of Wesley's *A Plain Account of Christian Per-*

---

[1] John Wesley, questioned by Dr. Rutherford in 1768; quoted in J. M. Todd,
John Wesley and the Catholic Church, pp. 131 ff.

fection there is an interesting passage concerning receiving *and restoring* God's grace.[1] The idea appears frequently in the Wesley hymns. It appears that when we are aware of God's favour we should 'freely relinquish it' immediately, give it back to him, or else it will go bad on us. There is a danger in resting in God's favour. There must be a return; the circuit of giving and receiving must be kept intact to carry the current of love. The insight is not confined to Christianity. Virginia Woolf's Mrs. Dalloway did not for a moment believe in God but felt all the more that one must repay in daily life, 'one must pay back from this secret deposit of exquisite moments'.[2] But in the Christian way of life thanking and offering belong to one another organically.

And of course no one has counted up the ways human beings can be deceived about God and their spiritual condition. 'God tenders me the situation to which I have to answer; but I have not to expect that he should tender me anything of my answer. Certainly in my answering I am given into the power of his grace, but I cannot measure heaven's share in it, and even the most blissful sense of grace can deceive.'[3]

Incidentally, when the deception is recognized it can be the occasion of an advancing religious conviction and not merely one of disturbing doubt. In the work of sifting one's experiences and giving them their right names we sometimes realize that we have in fact been deceived, that what we thought was God was not him, not because we know who and what he is but because we know that this thing in our minds was a personal construct to fulfil our own wishes. But this can be spiritually productive:

> To reject this idol may often involve falling back upon scepticism, but sometimes one seems fleetingly to be enabled to reject the idol in the name of a Being who really is Another, who requires one to stop putting words into His mouth, Who has the unpredictable disconcerting quality of the God of the New Testament. . . . Who is to say that He is not another idol? At least He is a more subtle and convincing one.[4]

[1] John Wesley, op. cit., pp. 126, 128.
[2] Virginia Woolf, *Mrs. Dalloway*, pp. 33–4 (Penguin Edition).
[3] Martin Buber, *Between Man and Man* (publ. Kegan Paul), p. 69.
[4] Helen Oppenheimer, from an essay titled 'The Identifying of Grace' in *Theology*, February 1965, p. 80.

Assurance and the summons to sanctity together form the polarity of trust and mistrust which seems to be authentic Christian experience. We are not supposed to attempt any resolution of this complex situation. We are meant to be continually encouraged and discouraged, and to hope in God. For long enough Christians have been taught that one sins against hope in two ways, by presumption and by despair. We avoid despair by remembering God's mercy; we avoid presumption by taking a serious view of sin and realizing that all our attempts to conceal the truth about ourselves are about as effective as the Emperor's new clothes. St. Augustine summed up this polarity with admirable thoroughness: 'If there is no joy, there is defect in us: if we feel wholly safe, we exult wrongly.'[1]

Once we have come to the end of the beginning and have got into our stride in the life of faith we shall find that the image of a dark night which St. John of the Cross chose for the life of faith is the right one. But there is much mediated grace in this night. There is a certain inductive assurance which comes from observing the guided quality which the past mysteriously reveals when scrutinized by faith. There is a conviction that life is being handled less agitatedly and more affectionately, and accordingly, there is the developing realization that it is good to live life this way. There is the grace that keeps us in the continued confession of the apostolic faith and in the regular worship of the Church, there is the grace of a discontent with the self that nevertheless does not depress; and there is the grace that incredibly summons to perfection human beings who all have feet of clay. There is eucharistic grace with its load of assurance, of God's favour, of our membership in the mystical Body, of our title to the incorruptible Kingdom. And from his fullness we have received it all, grace upon grace.

But all this grace comes through faith alone, that is to say, through Christian faith's characteristic interpretation of experience. Sometimes faith confidently and easily interprets experience as from God; sometimes only slowly and after much argument with itself and life. And sometimes it simply has to hold on, like the troubled wrestler by the dark river, trusting that when the light breaks it will appear that the imagined enemy was Love all the time.

[1] St. Augustine, *Sermon on Psalm 85. 16.*

Acknowledgements

The authors and publishers are indebted to the following for permission to use material which originally appeared under their auspices:

The SCM Press Ltd for extracts from *The Existence of God* by H. Gollwitzer, and *The Primal Vision* by John V. Taylor.

Messrs. Routledge and Kegan Paul for the extracts from *Waiting on God* by Simone Weil, and *The Concept of Prayer* by D. Z. Phillips.

The Cambridge University Press for the quotation from *Soundings* (ed. Vidler) by H. E. Root.

Messrs. Longmans, Green & Co. Ltd., for an extract from *The Vision of God* by K. E. Kirk.

The Faith Press for permission to quote from D. E. Jenkins and G. B. Caird's *Jesus and God*.

Messrs. Sheed & Ward Ltd. for quotations from F. J. Sheed's translation of *The Confessions of St. Augustine* and Dom John Chapman's *Spiritual Letters*.

Messrs. Macmillan & Co. Ltd. for the extract from *Sprightly Running* by John Wain.

Messrs. Faber & Faber Ltd. for extracts from 'In Memory of Sigmund Freud' from *Collected Shorter Poems* by W. H. Auden.

The Marvell Press for the quotation from 'Church Going' by Philip Larkin from *The Less Deceived*.

Messrs. Hamish Hamilton Ltd. for the passage from *The Plague* by Albert Camus, translated by Stuart Gilbert.

The Hogarth Press Ltd. for the extract from *An Autobiography* by Edwin Muir.